CYCLING LA VÉLODYSSÉE

EUROVELO 1: ATLANTIC COAST OF FRANCE FROM BRITTANY TO HENDAYE

by Jack Jackson

JUNIPER HOUSE, MURLEY MOSS,
OXENHOLME ROAD, KENDAL, CUMBRIA LA9 7RL
cicerone.co.uk

First edition 2026
ISBN: 978 1 78631 274 7
eISBN: 978 1 78765 265 1

Printed in Czechia on behalf of Latitude Press Ltd on responsibly sourced paper.
A catalogue record for this book is available from the British Library.
All photographs are by the author unless otherwise stated.

Route mapping by Lovell Johns lovelljohns.com
Contains OpenStreetMap.org data © OpenStreetMap contributors, CC-BY-SA. NASA relief data courtesy of ESRI. Please be aware that the maps in this guide were created using open-source data and have not undergone the checking procedures of an official mapping agency.

Cicerone's EU representative for GPSR compliance is Easy Access System Europe, Mustamäe tee 50, 10621 Tallinn, Estonia. Email gpsr.requests@easproject.com.

Updates to this guide

While we strive to ensure that our guidebooks are as up to date and accurate as possible, changes can occur during the lifetime of an edition. Facilities, accommodation, transport and even rights of way can change, so if you find any inaccuracies in this book or have any feedback, please let us know by email at updates@cicerone.co.uk. Updates will be published on the Cicerone website (cicerone.co.uk/1274/updates), so please check before planning your trip.

To receive free updates, special offers and GPX files where available, don't forget to **register** your book at the 'My Account' tab at cicerone.co.uk.

Front cover: Approaching the mouth of the river Bidassoa in Hendaye with less than 10km of La Vélodyssée to go

CONTENTS

ROUTE SUMMARY TABLE

Stage	Start	Finish	Time	Distance (km)	Ascent (m)	Descent (m)	Page
Brittany							
1	Roscoff	Carhaix-Plouguer	6hr 30min	79.9	790	660	41
2	Carhaix-Plouguer	Mûr-de-Bretagne	3hr 45min	64.3	360	350	49
3	Mûr-de-Bretagne	Josselin	3hr 45min	72	220	330	55
4	Josselin	Redon	3hr 50min	62.8	180	210	61
5	Redon	Nort-sur-Erdre	4hr 25min	72.5	110	110	67
6	Nort-sur-Erdre	Nantes	2hr 30min	38.7	200	200	74
Section 1 total			*24hr 50min*	*390.2*	*1860*	*1860*	
Pays de la Loire, Vendée and Charente-Maritime							
7	Nantes	Saint-Brevin-les-Pins	3hr 45min	61.3	180	180	83
8	Saint-Brevin-les-Pins	Bouin	4hr 35min	76.8	330	330	90
9	Bouin	Saint-Gilles-Croix-de-Vie	4hr 30min	72.6	130	130	97
10	Saint-Gilles-Croix-de-Vie	La Tranche-sur-Mer	5hr 10min	81.5	240	240	102
11	La Tranche-sur-Mer	La Rochelle	3hr 45min	71.5	80	80	109
12	La Rochelle	Rochefort	2hr 35min	50	120	120	116
13	Rochefort	Royan	4hr 40min	83.7	260	260	121
Section 2 total			*29hr*	*497.4*	*1340*	*1340*	
Aquitaine							
14	Royan	Lacanau-Océan	4hr 40min	84.3	260	250	129
15	Lacanau-Océan	Arcachon	4hr	80.1	130	140	135
16	Arcachon	Gastes	3hr 35min	66.2	300	280	141
17	Gastes	Léon	4hr	70.4	250	250	147
18	Léon	Bayonne	3hr	61.9	130	150	152
19	Bayonne	Hendaye	3hr	51.7	490	490	160
Section 3 total			*22hr 15min*	*414.6*	*1560*	*1560*	
La Vélodyssée total			**76hr**	**1302.2**	**4760**	**4760**	

STAGE FACILITIES PLANNER

Stage	Place	Altitude	Time	Distance	Facility
1	**Roscoff**	**6m**	-	-	ATM i
	Saint-Pol-de-Léon	39m	30min	6.4km	ATM i
	Morlaix	15m	2hr 35min	31.4km	ATM i
	Carhaix-Plouguer	**130m**	**6hr 30min**	**79.9km**	ATM i
2	Gouarec	134m	2hr 40min	46km	ATM
	L'Abbaye de Bon-Repos	129m	3hr	51km	
	Mûr-de-Bretagne	**140m**	**3hr 45min**	**64.3km**	ATM i
3	Pontivy	55m	1hr 15min	23.4km	ATM i
	Rohan	67m	2hr 30min	47.8km	ATM
	Josselin	**34m**	**3hr 45min**	**72km**	ATM i
4	Le Roc-Saint-André	22m	1hr	16.9km	ATM
	Malestroit	15m	1hr 35min	25.5km	ATM i
	Saint-Congard	8m	2hr 5min	34.1km	ATM
	Saint-Martin-sur-Oust	6m	2hr 30min	40.3km	

general accommodation · camping · refreshments · shop · bike shop · ATM · info · train · bus

Stage	Place	Altitude	Time	Distance	Facility
	Le Pont d'Oust	7m	2hr 45min	45.6km	camping, refreshments
	Painfaut	11m	3hr 15min	53.3km	camping, refreshments
	Redon	**3m**	**3hr 50min**	**62.8km**	general accommodation, camping, refreshments, shop, bike shop, ATM, info, train
5	Guenrouet	3m	1hr 25min	22.7km	camping, refreshments, shop, ATM
	Blain	12m	2hr 45min	45.2km	general accommodation, camping, refreshments, shop, bike shop, ATM
	Nort-sur-Erdre	**5m**	**4hr 30min**	**72.5km**	general accommodation, camping, refreshments, shop, bike shop, ATM, info, train
6	Sucé-sur-Erdre	7m	1hr 15min	20km	refreshments, shop
	Nantes	**5m**	**3hr 30min**	**38.7km**	general accommodation, camping, refreshments, shop, bike shop, ATM, info, train, bus
7	Le Pellerin	6m	1hr 30min	24km	general accommodation, refreshments, shop
	Le Migron	2m	2hr 20min	38.2km	general accommodation, refreshments
	Paimboeuf	5m	2hr 55min	48km	general accommodation, camping, refreshments, shop, bike shop, ATM
	Saint-Brevin-les-Pins	**3m**	**3hr 45min**	**61.3km**	general accommodation, camping, refreshments, shop, bike shop, ATM, info
8	Saint-Michel-Chef-Chef	27m	45min	11.8km	refreshments, shop, bike shop, ATM

Stage	Place	Altitude	Time	Distance	Facility
	Préfailles	9m	1hr 25min	24.2km	
	Pornic	4m	2hr 25min	40.2km	ATM i
	Les Moutiers-en-Retz	5m	3hr 20min	55.5km	ATM i
	Bouin	**4m**	**4hr 35min**	**76.8km**	ATM i
9	*L'Île de Noirmoutier (Variant)*	*1m*	*30min*	*7.7km*	ATM i
	Beauvoir-sur-Mer	7m	1hr	16.6km	ATM i
	Fromentine	2m	2hr 10min	35.5km	i
	Saint-Jean-de-Monts	3m	3hr 20min	54.6km	ATM i
	Saint-Gilles-Croix-de-Vie	**2m**	**4hr 30min**	**72.6km**	ATM i
10	Les Sables-d'Olonne	2m	2hr 20min	37.1km	ATM i
	Jard-sur-Mer	10m	3hr 55min	62.8km	ATM i
	La Tranche-sur-Mer	**2m**	**5hr 10min**	**81.5km**	ATM i
11	L'Aiguillon-sur-Mer	3m	30min	9.4km	ATM i
	Saint-Michel-en-l'Herm	2m	1hr 15min	23.8km	ATM
	Marans	2m	2hr 30min	46.2km	ATM

Stage	Place	Altitude	Time	Distance	Facility
	La Rochelle	**5m**	**3hr 45min**	**71.5km**	ATM
12	Châtelaillon-Plage	2m	40min	13.7km	ATM
	Saint-Laurent-de-la-Prée	5m	1hr 30min	29.7km	ATM
	Rochefort	**2m**	**2hr 35min**	**50km**	ATM
13	Saint-Agnant	6m	1hr 5min	20.3km	ATM
	Marennes	16m	1hr 55min	35.2km	ATM
	Ronce-les-Bains	4m	2hr 30min	45.2km	ATM
	La Palmyre	4m	3hr 40min	65.8km	ATM
	Royan	**3m**	**4hr 40min**	**83.7km**	ATM
14	Soulac-sur-Mer	4m	30min	8.4km	ATM
	Plage du Gurp	15m	1hr 5min	20.4km	
	Montalivet-les-Bains	8m	1hr 40min	29.7km	ATM
	Plage du Pin Sec	18m	2hr 30min	44.6km	
	Hourtin Plage	18m	2hr 45min	49.7km	
	Carcans Plage (off route)	*16m*	*3hr 40min*	*66.5km*	

Stage	Place	Altitude	Time	Distance	Facility
	Maubuisson (off route)	*17m*	*3hr 50min*	*69.8km*	
	Lacanau-Océan	**9m**	**4hr 40min**	**84.3km**	ATM
15	Le Porge-Océan	7m	40min	13km	
	Le Grand Crohot	9m	1hr 15min	24.3km	
	Andernos-les-Bains	10m	2hr	40.5km	ATM
	Audenge	13m	2hr 30min	50.2km	
	Biganos	15m	2hr 50min	56.6km	ATM
	Arcachon	**5m**	**4hr**	**80.1km**	ATM
16	Dune du Pilat	36m	35min	10.2km	
	Biscarrosse Plage	15m	1hr 45min	32.5km	ATM
	Navarrosse	22m	2hr 10min	43.1km	
	Biscarrosse	26m	2hr 35min	48.8km	ATM
	Parentis-en-Born	30m	3hr 5min	57.8km	ATM
	Gastes	**22m**	**3hr 35min**	**66.3km**	
17	Sainte-Eulalie-en-Born	28m	30min	8.3km	
	Mimizan Plage	3m	1hr 20min	23.5km	ATM

Stage	Place	Altitude	Time	Distance	Facility
	Contis Plage	12m	2hr 15min	39.1km	ATM
	Cap de l'Homy	15m	2hr 40min	46.7km	
	Saint-Girons-Plage	10m	3hr 15min	56.6km	
	Léon	**17m**	**4hr**	**70.4km**	ATM i
18	Moliets-et-Maa	17m	15min	5.4km	
	Messanges	10m	30min	9.4km	
	Vieux-Boucau-les-Bains	4m	40min	13.6km	
	Le Penon	3m	1hr 20min	27.6km	
	Hossegor	3m	1hr 30min	30.7km	ATM i
	Labenne-Océan	4m	2hr 5min	41km	
	Bayonne	**7m**	**3hr**	**61.9km**	ATM i
19	Biarritz	14m	40min	11.7km	ATM i
	Bidart	51m	1hr 10min	20.3km	
	Guéthary	30m	1hr 20min	22.8km	i
	Saint-Jean-de-Luz	3m	1hr 50min	30.9km	ATM i
	Hendaye	**3m**	**3hr**	**51.7km**	ATM i

OVERVIEW PROFILE/ALTERNATIVE SCHEDULES

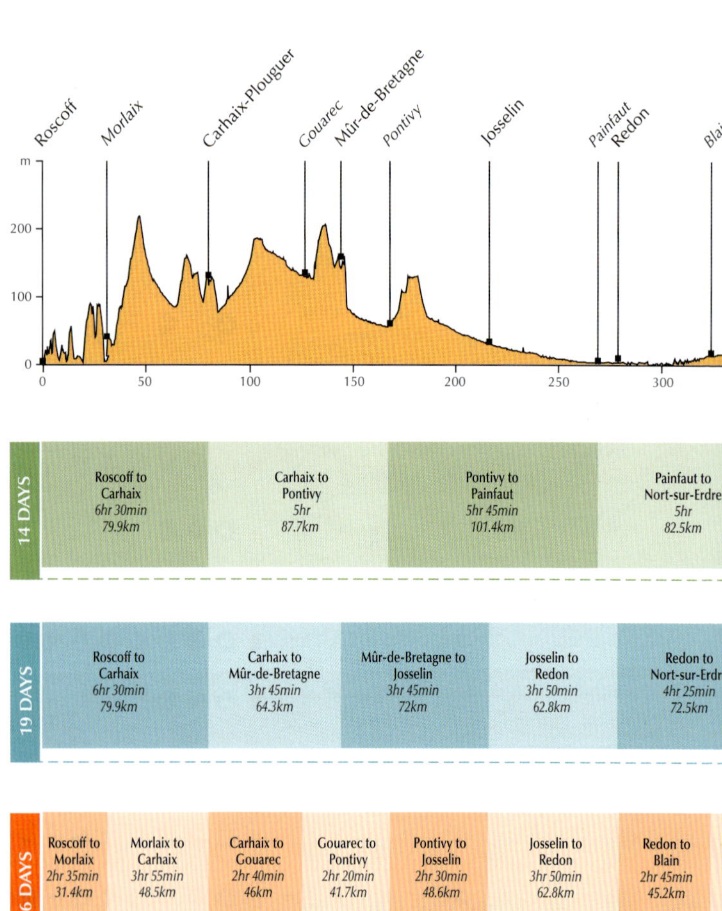

Stages marked with * miss out the stage finish in Bouin, reducing the overall distance by 5.6km.

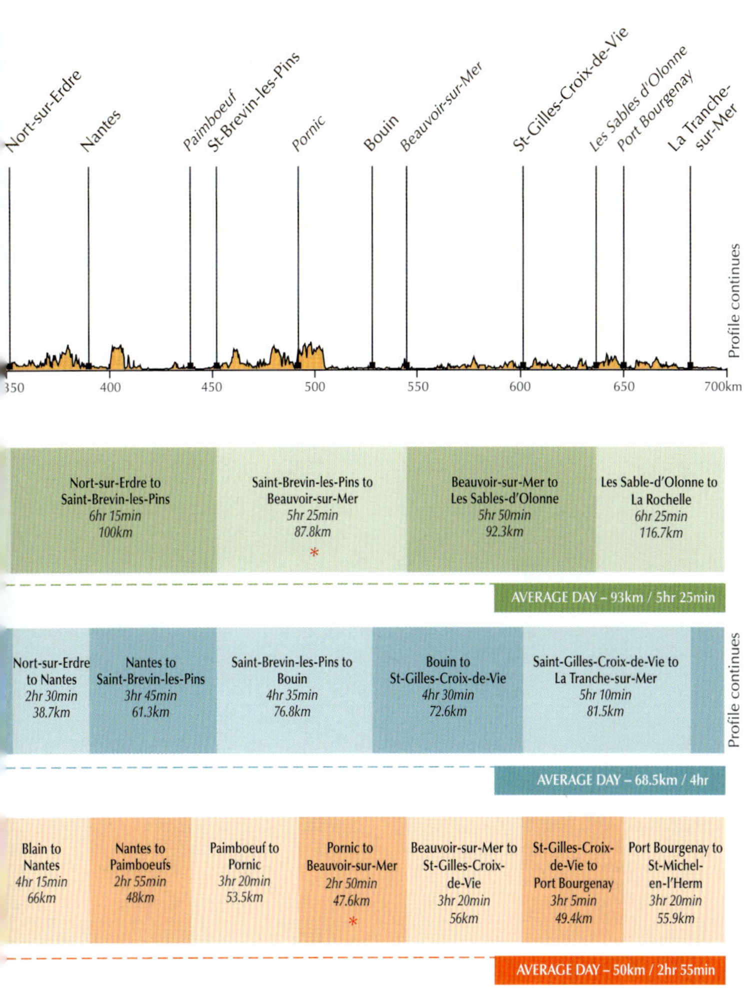
Nort-sur-Erdre
Nantes
Paimboeuf
St-Brevin-les-Pins
Pornic
Bouin
Beauvoir-sur-Mer
St-Gilles-Croix-de-Vie
Les Sables d'Olonne
Port Bourgenay
La Tranche-sur-Mer
Profile continues
350
400
450
500
550
600
650
700km
Nort-sur-Erdre to Saint-Brevin-les-Pins 6hr 15min 100km
Saint-Brevin-les-Pins to Beauvoir-sur-Mer 5hr 25min 87.8km *
Beauvoir-sur-Mer to Les Sables-d'Olonne 5hr 50min 92.3km
Les Sable-d'Olonne to La Rochelle 6hr 25min 116.7km
AVERAGE DAY – 93km / 5hr 25min
Nort-sur-Erdre to Nantes 2hr 30min 38.7km
Nantes to Saint-Brevin-les-Pins 3hr 45min 61.3km
Saint-Brevin-les-Pins to Bouin 4hr 35min 76.8km
Bouin to St-Gilles-Croix-de-Vie 4hr 30min 72.6km
Saint-Gilles-Croix-de-Vie to La Tranche-sur-Mer 5hr 10min 81.5km
Profile continues
AVERAGE DAY – 68.5km / 4hr
Blain to Nantes 4hr 15min 66km
Nantes to Paimboeufs 2hr 55min 48km
Paimboeuf to Pornic 3hr 20min 53.5km
Pornic to Beauvoir-sur-Mer 2hr 50min 47.6km *
Beauvoir-sur-Mer to St-Gilles-Croix-de-Vie 3hr 20min 56km
St-Gilles-Croix-de-Vie to Port Bourgenay 3hr 5min 49.4km
Port Bourgenay to St-Michel-en-l'Herm 3hr 20min 55.9km
AVERAGE DAY – 50km / 2hr 55min

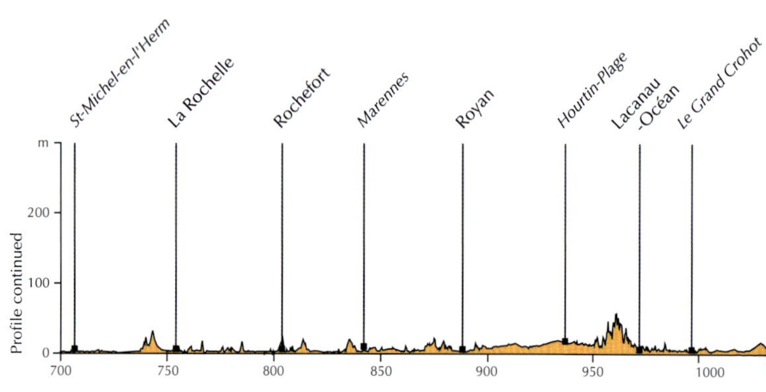

Les Sable-d'Olonne to La Rochelle *6hr 25min* *116.7km*	La Rochelle to LMarennes *4hr 30min* *88.4km*	Marennes to Hourtin Plage *5hr 30min* *95km*	Hourtin Plage to Arcachon *5hr 55min* *114.7km*

Profile continued

La Tranche-sur-Mer to La Rochelle *3hr 45min* *71.5km*	La Rochelle to Rochefort *2hr 35min* *50km*	Rochefort to Royan *4hr 40min* *83.7km*	Royan to Lacanau-Océan *4hr 40min* *84.3km*	Lacanau-Océan to Arcachon *4hr* *80.1km*

St-Michel-en-l'Herm to La Rochelle *2hr 30min* *47.7km*	La Rochelle to Rochefort *2hr 35min* *50km*	Rochefort to Marennes *1hr 55min* *38.4km*	Marennes to Royan *2hr 45min* *45.3km*	Royan to Hourtin Plage *2hr 45min* *49.7km*	Hourtin to Le Grand Crohot *3hr 10min* *58.9km*	Le Grand Crohot to Arcachon *2hr 45min* *55.8km*

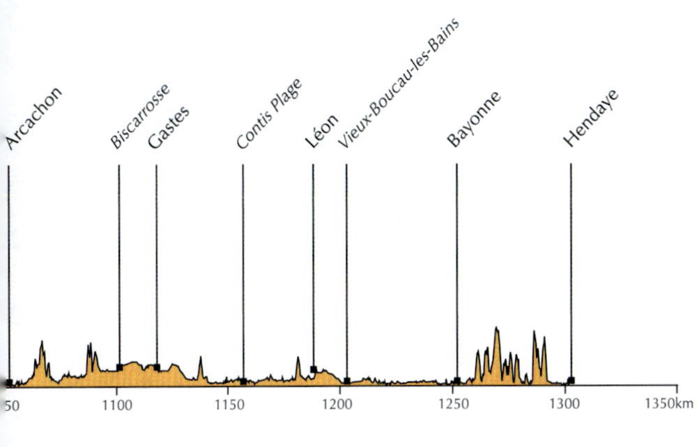
Arcachon
Biscarrosse
Gastes
Contis Plage
Léon
Vieux-Boucau-les-Bains
Bayonne
Hendaye
50
1100
1150
1200
1250
1300
1350km

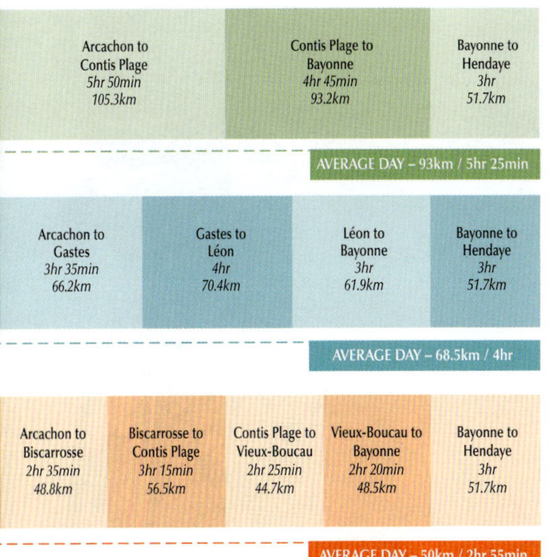
Arcachon to Contis Plage 5hr 50min 105.3km
Contis Plage to Bayonne 4hr 45min 93.2km
Bayonne to Hendaye 3hr 51.7km
AVERAGE DAY – 93km / 5hr 25min
Arcachon to Gastes 3hr 35min 66.2km
Gastes to Léon 4hr 70.4km
Léon to Bayonne 3hr 61.9km
Bayonne to Hendaye 3hr 51.7km
AVERAGE DAY – 68.5km / 4hr
Arcachon to Biscarrosse 2hr 35min 48.8km
Biscarrosse to Contis Plage 3hr 15min 56.5km
Contis Plage to Vieux-Boucau 2hr 25min 44.7km
Vieux-Boucau to Bayonne 2hr 20min 48.5km
Bayonne to Hendaye 3hr 51.7km
AVERAGE DAY – 50km / 2hr 55min

A medieval street in the centre of Malestroit (Stage 4)

INTRODUCTION

Château de Blain (Stage 5)

La Vélodyssée is a 1300km cycling odyssey along the Atlantic coast of France. The waymarked route, much of it on dedicated cycle paths, forms the French section of the European Atlantic Coast Route, EuroVelo 1, which runs along the western edge of Europe, from Norway to Portugal. The route takes you through three regions of France that capture both the essence of the country and its considerable variety, travelling through agricultural landscapes and iconic gastronomic regions and along stunning coastline. If you're excited by the idea of multi-day bike adventures, La Vélodyssée is for you. At 1300km it offers a challenge for experienced long-distance cycle tourers, but as the route is relatively flat and has a high proportion of traffic-free trails, it makes it a pleasure for cyclists of any level. Not all cycle tourists have two or three weeks to dedicate to a tour. Fortunately, the two major river estuaries of the Loire and the Gironde naturally divide La Vélodyssée into three 1-week-long tours. These three sections each have distinctive characteristics and form rewarding tours.

You start at the Channel port of Roscoff on the north coast of Brittany, following the course of a disused railway to cross the region's agricultural uplands. Then on the towpath of the Nantes–Brest canal, you contour through bustling medieval towns and past ancient castles to arrive on the banks of the river Loire. The wild Atlantic coast now accompanies you all the way to the Basque Country and the Spanish border: first through the drained marshland of Loire Maritime, Vendée and Charente, including the historic ports of La Rochelle, Rochefort and Royan; then, having crossed the wide river Gironde estuary by ferry, you weave your way through massive undulating sand dunes and pine forests, alongside world-class surfing beaches, before reaching the glitzy resorts of south-west France.

Bernard Hinault statue in the centre of Carhaix (Stage 1)

WHY LA VÉLODYSSÉE?

La Vélodyssée is one of the longest fully signposted cycle routes in France, with 80% of the route on traffic-free paths. It is served by high-quality transport links and an abundance and wide range of accommodation to suit all tastes and budgets.

The route travels through regions that have some of the best tourism infrastructure in Europe, with much of it centred on outdoor activities. There are plenty of places to stay along the way, with accommodation options ranging from budget campsites to luxurious hotels in former palaces. France also offers some of the best dining opportunities in the world, and cyclists on La Vélodyssée find no shortage of delicious regional food to choose from. If you enjoy beach life, much of the route is adjacent to beaches of soft golden sands, popular with both families and serious surfers.

Cycle touring is inherently an environmentally friendly form of travel. Arriving in Roscoff by boat at the start of La Vélodyssée and leaving the finish at Hendaye by train not only adds to the adventure of the odyssey but also minimises the impact of your journey on the environment.

For those in search of a longer adventure, La Vélodyssée intersects with other multi-day cycle routes (see Appendix D). It is part of the EuroVelo 1, which runs for 11,000km from North Cape in Norway to Sagres in Portugal. La Vélodyssée joins the River Loire Cycle Route at Nantes, and you can connect the Atlantic to the Mediterranean via the Canal des Deux Mers route, starting at Royan. A day's ride from the end of La Vélodyssée takes you to Saint-Jean-Pied-de-Port, the start of the Camino de Santiago across northern Spain. There is also a vast web of regional waymarked cycleways linking with La Vélodyssée, allowing numerous ways to personalise your adventure.

WHEN TO RIDE

It is possible to cycle La Vélodyssée all year round, although it provides particularly great cycling conditions in the spring, summer and autumn. As the route travels south, the average temperatures are 3–4°C warmer on Stage 19 compared with Stage 1. Temperatures in Biarritz are in the mid-twenties in July, August and September and in the high teens in May, June and October. All the campsites, restaurants and hotels along the route are open during this period, and the proximity of beautiful beaches to much of the route makes April to October the ideal time for cycling La Vélodyssée.

Unpacking kit on arrival at a campsite

Lower temperatures, stronger winds, more frequent rain and the closure of some of the seasonal holiday infrastructure make the winter a less attractive season for La Vélodyssée for all but the hardiest of cycle tourers.

CHOOSING YOUR SCHEDULE

The stages of this guide are based on taking 19 days to complete the route, cycling approximately 75km per day. This also means that the three geographical sections of the route each take about a week, enabling the whole of La Vélodyssée to be cycled on three separate 1-week tours.

The end of most stages offers a range of facilities, including, campsites, hotels, shops, cafés and restaurants. An attempt is made to include a range of each in the guide, but this list is far from exhaustive. On some stages, accommodation options are so ubiquitous that it is hard to choose between them. On a few, such as Stage 8, if you are in search of a particular type of accommodation that is not available at the end of the stage, you may choose to extend or finish the stage early. The 'Stage facilities planner' at the beginning of this guide offers help with your planning.

Several websites providing information about low-cost or free accommodation along the route are available. One of the best of these is Warm Showers (warmshowers.org): a contact-sharing site where fellow cyclists offer free accommodation to cycle tourists, ranging from camping in their garden to a spare room.

For most cyclists all stages will require 3–6hr of cycling per day. As this will not suit all cyclists, two additional itineraries are provided in the 'Alternative schedules' graphic at the beginning of this guide. One averages 50km per day, taking four weeks to complete the route, and the other averages 95km per day, taking two weeks in total. For most of the route it would be possible to personalise the itineraries further, although there are some sections where it would be difficult to find a full range of facilities.

For less experienced cycle tourists, it is a good idea to do a few day rides, increasing them in length to find the daily distance that suits you and can be sustained for multiple days.

GETTING THERE AND BACK

By sea

Roscoff can be reached conveniently by sea from the UK and Ireland, with operator Brittany Ferries carrying bikes at no extra charge. From Plymouth in the UK, sailings run between April and November either in the afternoon, taking 5hr, or overnight. You disembark an overnight crossing in time to start Stage 1; afternoon crossings arrive in Roscoff in the evening. From Cork in Ireland, a 15hr afternoon sailing runs from March to October on Saturdays and Wednesdays. Arrival into Roscoff is the following morning.

By air

The nearest airport to the start of La Vélodyssée is Brest (half an hour from Morlaix by train), which has flights to Paris Charles de Gaulle Airport (CDG) and from there to the rest of the world.

Bikes will need to be disassembled and packed in clear-plastic bike bags or cardboard boxes. Check with your carrier, as conditions can vary between airlines.

By rail

Roscoff station closed in 2018 following a landslide that blocked the track, and it is unclear if it will be reopened. A replacement bus service carrying bikes operates from Morlaix.

A direct TGV train runs from Paris-Montparnasse to Morlaix, taking about 3hr. Bikes are carried for a fee in a reservable bike space. These can be booked when you buy your train ticket, but there are usually only two per train. Bikes can be transported for free if disassembled and packed to a maximum size of 130cm x 90cm.

It is possible to get from the UK to Morlaix by train, via Paris, in under

Dedicated bike transport on a TGV train

8hr. Eurostar trains from London St Pancras to Paris-Gare-du-Nord take disassembled bikes, packed in a bike box or a purpose-made bike bag, providing you have a bike reservation. Eurostar is exploring the ability to accept fully assembled bikes in future (see help.eurostar.com).

Local TER train services, such as Saint-Brieuc to Morlaix, have mandatory bookings for bikes from 1 May to 30 September. You need to go to the specific BreizhGo page (breizhgo.bzh) to book bikes, which is done separately from passenger bookings. There is a small fee but a much larger on-the-spot fine if you haven't booked your bike in advance.

By bus

Bus services operate to Morlaix from Paris; the journey takes about 8hr and can offer a cost-effective way of getting to Roscoff. Bikes will usually need to be fully disassembled. As buses are not ideal for carrying bikes, services are only marked on the book maps and tables at key points for access and onward connections.

Intermediate access

If you are breaking La Vélodyssée into three sections, Nantes and Royan are natural access points. Nantes is 2hr from Paris by TGV and has an international airport with direct flights to most European countries. Royan is 4hr from Paris by train and 2hr from La Rochelle. For those breaking La Vélodyssée into two sections, trains from Les Sables-d'Olonne take 4hr to Paris and 90min to Nantes.

Getting home

Hendaye is 5hr from Paris by TGV and 10hr from London via Paris using Eurostar. For those looking to end their journey by sea, Bilbao is 160km by bike, or 2hr by bus, from the end of La Vélodyssée. Brittany Ferries sails from Bilbao to Portsmouth twice a week between April and November; and twice a week year-round to Rosslare in Ireland.

Bilbao airport (BIO) has flights to most European countries. Closer to Hendaye, San Sebastián Airport (EAS) is a flat 5km ride and has direct flights to Madrid, a major hub for onward international flights, and UK airports.

FOOD AND DRINK

Where to eat

For most of the route there is an abundance of places to eat, ranging from roadside cafés to Michelin-starred restaurants. Some of these facilities are listed in the stage descriptions, but this is far from exhaustive. Even small French villages will most likely have at least one bakery (boulangerie); these are ideal places to purchase bread and pastries to enjoy on the beaches, benches and picnic tables along the route.

When to eat

Breakfast (petit-déjeuner), whether eaten in a hotel, café or bakery, usually consists of freshly baked bread and pastries served with coffee and fruit juice.

At lunchtime (déjeuner), cafés and restaurants, often with tables spilling out onto the pavement outside, will usually offer a lunch menu (a set meal for a fixed price). This is often good value, particularly if it includes a dish of the day (plat du jour). If you are looking for an al fresco lunch beside the route, a picnic can also be sourced at the boulangerie, with savoury pastries or a baguette filled with cheese or charcuterie.

Outside the bakery in Mûr-de-Bretagne (Stage 2)

Many restaurants advertise their evening meal (diner) with both fixed-price and à la carte menus. In the bigger towns and cities, there is a cosmopolitan choice of dining, although in smaller towns and villages, restaurants will traditionally offer French cuisine using locally sourced ingredients. There is often also a pizzeria.

What to eat

Cooking and eating are a fundamental part of French culture, and it would be possible to write a book the size of this guide just dedicated to excellent food found along the route. In virtually every dining establishment, other than international chains, you can expect food to be freshly prepared and cooked to a high standard, whether in a quiet bistro or a fine-dining restaurant. Local food specialities along La Vélodyssée can be divided into the three sections: Brittany to the north of the Loire, the Basque influence south of the Gironde, and the coastal lowlands in between.

Cycling through Brittany, you will frequently pass grazing dairy cattle, so it is no surprise that much of the cuisine uses locally produced dairy products. Many Breton towns have a crêperie, which serves two types of the French pancake: the thin crêpe made with a sugared wheat flour and served with sweet fillings and the thicker savoury Breton galette made with buckwheat flour.

Breton patisseries (cake shops) will tempt you with sugary delights, such as kouign-amann, made from layers of butter, sugar and pastry and baked until crispy on the outside and soft in the centre; Far Breton, a dense custard cake with dried fruits; beignets Breton, deep-fried dough balls, like doughnuts; and the Paris–Brest, a round pastry filled with praline cream and topped with almonds, which was created to commemorate the bike race between the two cities.

The cuisine of the coastal marshland between the Loire and the Gironde is unsurprisingly dominated by the bounty from the sea. Moules-frites (mussels and chips) can be found on the menu at most seaside restaurants, and éclade de moules is a traditional Charente-Maritime dish where the mussels are laid in concentric circles then cooked under a cover of pine needles.

Marennes Oléron oysters are world renowned; they are usually served raw or with a squeeze of lemon and are available in most local restaurants as well as direct from the producers. Saint-Gilles-Croix-de-Vie has a thriving sardine industry, with some making their way directly to local restaurants; many more arrive at the historic La Perle des Dieux canning factory and are available to buy in colourful cans from the shop next to the route.

The cuisines of Vendée and Charente-Maritime are not only about the sea; two of the three most popular hams in France are produced along the route of La Vélodyssée, with jambon de Vendée taking the lower podium position. Popular on menus, it is paired with mogette de Vendée, a

A seafood platter; ratatouille salad; catch of the day

A 24-hour fresh-oyster vending machine at Port du Collet (Stage 8)

locally grown white bean. La Vendée also has a successful poultry farming industry and is the second-largest producer of foie gras in France. The loose sandy soil of Île de Noirmoutier is ideal for growing early La Bonnotte potatoes, which appear on some of the finest menus.

South of the Gironde estuary you enter the Basque Country, where livestock farming forms a significant part of the economy and is reflected in the local cuisine. Kintoa pork from the local Pie Noir du Pays Basque pigs is used to make the jambon de Bayonne, the top of the podium for French ham. Axoa d'Espelette is a stew made with minced veal and chillis, and zikiro is a suckling lamb barbecued vertically over a woodfire.

In the region's patisseries you will find colourful Saint-Jean-de-Luz macarons and the gâteau Basque (Basque cake), typically filled with locally made black Itxassou cherry jam.

What to drink

The Loire and Gironde rivers, which divide La Vélodyssée into its three sections, are the two great wine-producing river valleys of western France. The region to the west of Nantes produces the dry, light-bodied Muscadet, which is made from the Melon de Bourgogne grape and described as the perfect pairing for oysters. Bordeaux produces over 700 million bottles of wine per year, ranging from large quantities of everyday table wine to some of the world's most expensive and prestigious bottles. Most of the production is red, called claret in the UK, but white, rosé and sparkling Bordeaux wines are also made.

Beer is also a popular drink in France, and a refreshing cold draft beer (une pression) from a beachside bar is a popular way to celebrate a long day on the bike. There are two types: blond (lager) and blanche (cloudy wheat beer). In Brittany, cidre (cider) is as popular as beer; cidre doux is light and sweet, cidre brut is dry and cidre demi-sec is in between.

Most regions of France produce a local aperitif or digestif (after-dinner drink). In Brittany, Pommeau de Bretagne is made by mixing unfermented apple juice with Calvados; in Charente, Pineau is produced by

Cycle tourist with traditional front and rear pannier setup

adding cognac to wine; and in the Basque region, Izarra is a distillate of plants and spices. If you were choosing only one of these to occupy the back of your drink's cabinet, Izarra is produced in Hendaye at the end of the route.

YOUR BIKE

Choosing the right type of bike

The best bike for cycling La Vélodyssée is the one you have. If you place bikes on a spectrum, with ultra-light road-racing bikes on one end, gravel and touring bikes in the middle and mountain bikes with large-travel full-suspension on the other, then all but the two extremes are suitable. Some of the tracks have stony or bumpy surfaces so are not ideal for narrow-tyred carbon wheels. Although it is not essential, you may enjoy a smoother ride with front suspension, but rear suspension will add a negligible level of comfort compared with the additional weight and extra energy it absorbs.

If you are choosing from a full range of bikes, then a modern gravel bike with a good range of gears, a lightweight frame, drop handlebars and a medium tyre width is the optimum choice. La Vélodyssée is very well suited to the use of e-bikes.

Preparing your bike

Whichever bike you take, it should be in good working order when you set off. For road bikes, fit the widest tyre they can accommodate, with a relatively good tread, and for mountain bikes the opposite: the narrowest tyres with the smallest knobbles.

There are relatively few mechanical traumas that a bike will experience without giving you advanced warning in the form of squeaks, rattles or judders. Getting these addressed early can prevent a bigger problem happening on the trail. There is a good provision of cycle shops along La Vélodyssée, and most will advise on any mechanical concerns and repair or replace parts if necessary.

Lightweight bike repair kit

Two problems that can sneak up unannounced, and which will halt your ride, are a puncture and a broken chain. Punctures are to be expected on a journey of this length but using tyres that are in good condition and made of puncture-resistant material can greatly reduce their likelihood. It is essential to carry a puncture-repair kit for your type of tyre. Carrying a spare innertube will save you time and effort.

Prevention of a broken chain is better than cure; consider fitting a new chain before you start your trip and always lubricate it at the start of each day. A link-extraction tool can save the day for a broken chain, but whatever you carry in your repair kit, make sure you know how to use it. The sandy trails and salty air will not be kind to your bike, so clean it when you can.

Bike shops are an excellent source of advice on preparing your bike for a trip like La Vélodyssée.

WHAT TO TAKE

Carrying your kit

Unless you are using a service that delivers your luggage to your destination, your bike will need to be capable of carrying your kit. Whichever bags you use, they should be waterproof or lined with waterproof plastic bags. There are essentially three options; which you choose will depend on the bike you are using and how much kit you take.

Laying out kit before packing

Lightweight bikepacking bags can be fixed to the seat post, cross bar and handlebar, using hook-and-loop straps; these don't require an additional carrier to mount, are more streamlined and have the least impact on the manoeuvrability of your bike.

Traditional panniers can be fitted around the front and rear wheel, using a rack fixed to the bike frame. In addition, a handlebar bag can be used to carry items that you want to access easily. Loaded panniers will reduce the stability and increase the width of your bike.

Bike trailers, carrying either children, pets or luggage, are common on the trail, particularly behind electric bikes. They can have one or two wheels and greatly increase your capacity to carry equipment but significantly reduce manoeuvrability.

Backpacks should not be used for carrying anything other than the lightest and smallest of equipment. It is better to use rear pockets on a jacket for items such as your phone, snacks or glasses. Some companies provide self-guided packages, including transporting your luggage from one stopover to the next.

Clothing and personal items

With the exceptions of the earlier and later stages, La Vélodyssée is predominantly flat, but it is still worth keeping the weight, and preferably the volume, of the items carried to a minimum. If you have cycle toured before, try to remember what you didn't use last time and, except for the emergency kit, leave it behind this time. If you are new to this type of travel, a good strategy is to lay out all your kit before you start packing and question if every item is essential. If you are torn choosing between two similar items, reach for the kitchen scales.

You will need two outfits: one for when you're cycling and one for when you're not. It is a good idea to wash your cycling kit each evening if possible. Layers are always preferable to a thick item of clothing, as they provide more options for different temperatures.

The kit you need to carry will also depend on your type of accommodation and plans for meals. Camping can reduce the cost and increase the self-sufficiency of your trip, but it will add weight and volume to your kit. If staying in smart hotels, you may choose to upgrade your non-cycling clothes. Appendix B offers a list of clothing, camping, cooking and essential personal items that you may need. Choosing the right kit can be a fun part of the adventure.

SAFETY AND EMERGENCIES

When using a road or cycleway, cycle on the right and take roundabouts anticlockwise. A cycle helmet should be considered essential, and lights and high-visibility clothing will increase motorists' awareness of you.

When cycling on shared-use cycleways, be aware of other cyclists and pedestrians and potentially their pets. Use your bell when approaching cyclists or pedestrians from behind. Showing consideration, and offering a friendly greeting, will make the journey more enjoyable for you and all other trail users.

In the unlikely event of an emergency, the number for the emergency services is 112; mobile coverage is good on most of the route. UK nationals require a Global Health Insurance Card (GHIC) to access state healthcare in France on the same basis as a French resident; EU nationals require a European Health Insurance Card (EHIC). Both can be applied for through governmental websites. Neither are a replacement for taking out travel insurance; when choosing yours, be aware that generic travel insurance may not cover the theft of, or damage to, your bike. For UK travellers, Cycling UK cyclinguk.org offers advice on insurance policies tailored to the needs of cycle tourists.

NAVIGATION

Waymarking

Waymarking on La Vélodyssée is generally very good. As the signage of cycleways is the responsibility of local authorities, you will see a variety of types of signs, but these are increasingly becoming more standardised. La Vélodyssée forms part of a transcontinental EuroVelo and also uses cycleways that are part of more local véloroutes (cycle paths), so you will often see a collection of logos on the same sign.

Typically, there are three types of logos. A green square with a white image of a cyclist is the generic sign for a cycleway; these are ubiquitous and care is needed to not simply follow them as they will not always be part of your route. A bright green square with a large square logo in the corner and a number inside a map of France is used to waymark a véloroute or voie verte (greenway). A blue square with a large logo in the corner and a number inside the EU circle of 12 gold stars is used to waymark a EuroVelo.

The waymarking to follow is the blue EuroVelo 1 square with the La Vélodyssée logo in the corner. There are two forms of the logo, but both are on an orange background and say La Vélodyssée.

A waymarking sign with logos for La Vélodyssée EuroVelo 1, the regional Vélocean cycle route and a generic cycleway

Maps

The whole route is available on a single map: IGN 924 Greenways and Cycle Routes of France, which has comprehensive coverage of véloroutes and voies vertes. It provides a useful overview of the route and is ideal for seeing how La Vélodyssée connects to other routes, but at a scale of 1:1,000,000, it is less useful for navigation. More practical maps for navigating the route are the IGN Top 100 and Michelin Local Maps of France.

With the waymarking, maps and stage descriptions in this guide, it is possible to complete the whole route without any additional maps, particularly if the GPX coordinates are also used.

Waymarking sign for a mixed-use path, with logos for La Vélodyssée EuroVelo 1 and Véloroute V92, La Flow Vélo

Michelin maps (1:150,000)

- 308 Finistère, Morbihan
- 316 Loire-Atlantique, Vendée
- 324 Charente, Charente-Maritime
- 335 Gironde, Landes
- 342 Hautes-Pyrénees, Pyrénées-Atlantique

IGN maps (1:100,000)

- D29 Finistère
- D56 Morbihan
- D44 Loire-Atlantique
- D85 Vendée
- D17 Charente-Maritime
- D33 Gironde
- D40 Landes
- D64 Pyrénées-Atlantique

USING THIS GUIDE

There are 19 stages, each covered by maps at a scale of 1:200,000, plus urban maps at 1:40,000 and overview maps of each of the three sections. GPX files for the stages of La Vélodyssée are free to download at cicerone.co.uk/1274 for anyone who has bought this guide. This route is also available in the Cicerone app on your phone, where you can download and view GPS-enabled maps for offline navigation, check route details and local points of interest.

For many stages, such as along the Brest–Nantes canal, navigation poses few challenges, but more attention is needed when approaching some urban areas. The route descriptions were accurate at the time of writing, but things can change; the route is regularly being upgraded and temporary diversions can be in place.

Bracketed distances are in kilometres, and times in hours and minutes. The first number is the cumulative distance from the start of the stage and the second the time from the start of the stage. Times will of course vary between cyclists and are offered as a guide only. The average speed used is approximately 17.5km/h, with slower or faster average speeds used for a particular stage, depending on the ascent, descent and distance of that stage.

Places that appear on the maps are shown in **bold** in the text. For each city, town or village on the route, a summary of the facilities available is provided, and the information box at the start of each stage identifies places along the route where you can find refreshments and/or accommodation. This is neither exhaustive nor does it guarantee a business still exists or is open all year. The 'Stage facilities planner' at the start of the book is provided to help you with day-to-day planning, while contact details for accommodation providers on the route appear in Appendix A (fuller lists of accommodation can be found on local tourist office websites).

Generally, in this guide 'cycle track' is used to describe a dedicated cycleway with an uneven surface, and 'cycle path' for one with a metalled surface. Both are often shared with pedestrians. 'Cycle lane' is used for a section of a road identified for cyclists, some separated from the main carriageway by a physical barrier and some simply by road markings. Some cycle lanes go in the opposite direction to vehicles on an otherwise one-way street; in this case, there will be a sauf vélo (except bikes) sign beneath the red circle with a white bar.

View between the viaduct's arches from the first level walkway in Morlaix (Stage 1)

HISTORY

On La Vélodyssée, you can experience the complete human history of France. Brittany and the western coast have seen migrations, invasions and conflicts involving Romans, Moors, Celts and Vikings. It has been the theatre for centuries of wars between France and Brittain and major battles in the two World Wars. All have left an impression on the landscape and culture, which is still there to experience today.

Early history

The coast of France has been inhabited since at least 7000BC, and evidence of its earlier settlers can be seen in monuments built by Neolithic people, such as the Menhir de la Pierre Attelée near Saint-Brevin-les-Pins and the Tumulus des Mousseaux at Pornic. During the Iron Age, Brittany was populated by Celtic Gauls and the region was known as Armorica, meaning land by the sea, and the forested inland area was known as Argoad.

The Romans

In the first century BC, Caesar destroyed the fleet of the Veneti, the most powerful tribe in Armorica, and occupied the region. Vineyards planted around Bordeaux, and salterns (pools in which salt water is left to evaporate to make salt) created near Royan, ensured that trade flourished along the Atlantic coast. At the beginning of the fifth century, Celts who had been driven out of Britain by the Angles and the Saxons began arriving in Armorica, renaming it Little Brittain, or Brittany, and establishing the distinctive Breton culture.

The Franks

Rome was eventually defeated in AD486 by the Franks under King Clovis I, who went on to defeat the Visigoths and take control of western France. During Charlemagne's reign in the first half of the ninth century, he created the Kingdom of Aquitaine and subjugated Brittany.

In 1137, Eleanor became duchess of Aquitaine and married Prince Louis VII, who became king when his father, King Louis VI, died shortly afterwards. She was queen of France for 15 years until her marriage was annulled and she married Henry II of England. When Eleanor died in 1204, the Duchy of Aquitaine was inherited by her son, King John of England, and so became part of the English realm, sowing the seeds for the Hundred Years' War.

The Hundred Years' War

When Charles IV of France died in 1328 without sons or brothers, his nearest male relative was Edward III of England. However, the French barons did not want an Englishman on the French throne and Philip of Valois, Charles' paternal cousin, was crowned King Philip VI. He decided that the Duchy of Aquitaine should become part of France again and so began the Hundred Years' War between France and England.

In 1415, King Henry V sailed from England with an army of about 10,500 men and laid siege to Harfleur. He found himself outmanoeuvred, low on supplies and fighting a much larger French army at Agincourt, but they stiffened their sinews, went once more into the breach and emerged victorious. The battle is dramatised in Shakespeare's *Henry V*. By 1428, England had gained the upper hand and laid siege to Orléans. A French force led by the 17-year-old Jeanne d'Arc (Joan of Arc), believing that she had a divine mission from God to expel the English from France, lifted the Siege of Orléans.

The French court

Anne of Brittany became Duchess of Brittany in 1488 and was determined to keep the region independent from the French crown. She signed the Treaty of Redon with Henry VII of England, which permitted English forces to fight alongside Bretons against France. They had limited success, and three years later Anne accepted defeat and married Charles VIII of France. When Charles died, Anne's daughter Claude ceded the Duchy of Brittany to France, where it has remained ever since.

The Wars of Religion

In the second half of the 16th century, France was gripped by a series of religious wars between Catholics and the Protestant Huguenots. The conflict is estimated to have cost up to four million French lives. In 1610, Henry IV was assassinated by a Catholic zealot and succeeded by his son Louis XIII, with Cardinal Richelieu becoming his chief minister in 1624. Richelieu set out to destroy Huguenot strongholds, besieging La Rochelle for 14 months and ordering the destruction of Blain Castle and the sacking of Royan.

When Louis XIV married Maria Theresa in 1660, she was accompanied to the tiny Isle of Pheasants at Hendaye by her father Philip IV of Spain and the entire Spanish court. At the start of Louis' record-breaking 72-year reign, he reduced the freedoms given to Huguenots, leading to many choosing to emigrate to Protestant countries.

In 1706, Nantes' shipowners began trading in enslaved people and were soon followed by those from La Rochelle. This terrible triangle of trade saw French goods shipped to Africa and exchanged for enslaved people, who were transported across the Atlantic to work on the colonial plantations of the Caribbean. The ships then returned to France with the sugar and coffee they had produced. At the height of the trade, the French were trafficking approximately 13,000 African people each year.

Revolutions and Napoleons

In 1789, the Storming of the Bastille started the French Revolution, creating the First Republic. Louis XVI and his wife Marie Antoinette were executed, monasteries and religious institutions were closed and castles and palaces became the property of the state. Three years later, a Catholic and Royal Army was formed by inhabitants of the Vendée. This started the brutal three-year-long Guerre de Vendée, resulting in the death of approximately half of the population of the region. Four thousand of the counter-revolutionaries, who had unsuccessfully tried to capture Nantes, were drowned in the river Loire.

The French First Republic lasted until the declaration of the First Empire on 18 May 1804, following the dismissal of the governing Directoire by Napoleon Bonaparte in 1799. After appointing himself emperor of the First French Empire, he set out to expand French territories across Europe. Napoleon was forced to retreat from Moscow in 1812, and three years later he was defeated by the Duke of Wellington at the Battle of Waterloo. As a result of the defeat, Napoleon abdicated in favour of his son, who became Napoleon II at the age of four, reigning for just two days. The First Empire came to an end with the coronation of King Louis XVIII in what became known as the Bourbon Restoration.

In 1830, the Second French Revolution overthrew the Bourbon monarch Charles X and replaced him with his cousin Louis-Philippe.

The Third French Revolution, in 1848, deposed Louis-Philippe and elected Louis Napoleon to be the first president of France. Four years later he declared himself emperor and he was crowned Napoleon III, exactly 48 years after the coronation of his uncle Napoleon I, and the Second French

Empire was born. Napoleon had Villa Eugénie built in Biarritz for the empress and initiated the planting of pine trees in the Landes. After French forces were defeated in the Franco-Prussian War in 1871, Napoleon was deposed by the Gouvernement de la Défense nationale and the Third Republic began.

La Belle Époque

La Belle Époque (Beautiful Era) refers to the period between the Franco-Prussian War and World War 1. It was a period of political stability, when the arts flourished, and much of western Europe experienced economic prosperity, and members of the European aristocracy established playgrounds for the wealthy, such as Biarritz and Saint-Jean-de-Luz. The increasing middle class, the expansion of the railways and a fashion for sea-bathing led to the growth of resorts with large seaside villas in many towns along the Atlantic coast.

A Belle Époque villa at Pontaillac (Stage 13)

Two World Wars

Growing tensions between European powers and treaties between their governments led to the unleashing of killing on an industrial scale in World War 1. By the time the Armistice was signed in 1918, the war had cost almost two million French lives. The interwar years saw an element of social reform and some towns flourished, but tensions between European nations remained, and Nazi Germany invaded and occupied France in 1940.

The French west coast was crucial to the Germans in the Battle of the Atlantic, and the German Navy was stationed at many ports. U-boats were used to attack the Atlantic convoys that were supplying Britain, and massive concrete submarine pens were built to house them at Bordeaux, La Rochelle and Saint-Nazaire. Allied commando attacks were launched, such as Operation Frankton in the Gironde, and hugely destructive air raids flattened Royan and severely damaged Nantes, resulting in a major loss of civilian life. The remains of German World War 2 structures can be found along La Vélodyssée, with some on clifftops and some gradually disappearing into sandy beaches.

Modern France

In 1951, France joined five other countries – Belgium, Germany, Italy, Luxembourg and the Netherlands – to initially create the European Coal and Steel Community, which became the European Economic Community six years later with the signing of the Treaty of Rome. The project progressed further in 1992, when the Maastricht Treaty created the European Union, and France and 10 other countries agreed to adopt a common currency, the Euro. In 2001, the first EuroVelo cycle route was created. By 2025, the European Union had 27 member countries, 9 were waiting to join and 1 had left.

NATURAL ENVIRONMENT

Brittany

On leaving the north coast, the route is characterised by wooded cycle paths and waterways, which provide a rich habitat for many plants and animals. The canal banks and surrounding trees are home to otters and horseshoe bats, while salmon, trout, eels and lamprey can be found in the water. They can be difficult to spot, but the beauty of the plant life and birds is hard to miss, including moorhens, mallards, herons, kingfishers, swallows and kestrels, which make their home along the canal.

On hot summer days, most cyclists will appreciate the shade provided by the ash, Scots pine, wild cherry, beech, oak, birch and walnut trees. But the most noticeable plants along the towpaths are the flowers at the lock-keeper's cottages, where scarlet poppies compete with vivid geraniums in window boxes.

Pays de la Loire, Vendée and Charente-Maritime

The Loire estuary is popular with birdwatchers drawn by the presence of many bird species, including warblers, sandpipers, curlews, storks, cranes, herons, plovers and terns. You will also meet people fishing along the banks of the canals, hoping to catch eel, carp, tench, perch or mullet.

Bordering the canals of the marais (marsh), you will find ash, elm, poplar, willow and alder trees, and flowering beneath them varieties of reeds, water lilies, bulrushes, irises, sedges, wild mint and angelica. The presence of field mice, rabbits, shrews and other small mammals encourage the raptors that feed on them, including kites, sparrowhawks, vultures, buzzards, harriers, kestrels and owls.

Most small creatures will hide themselves at the sound of your bike approaching, but the presence of otters can be identified by the small wakes they create as they swim silently through the water. The dry sunny summers and mild wet winters along the coast support mediterranean plant life and oceanic vegetation, including holm oak, strawberry trees, maritime pines, laurels and

Clockwise from top left: evergreen bugloss; poppies; lizard orchid; ragged robin; English stonecrop; broom rape; common mallow; beach morning

At the Grande Plage, Biarritz (Stage 19)

Andalusian firs. Colourful floral displays are created naturally by pyramid and lizard orchids, clematis, gorse and broom.

Aquitaine

The Landes de Gascogne is a landscape of pine forests and sand dunes, stretching along the Atlantic coast of Aquitaine. The forest was mostly planted over the last two hundred years to help stabilise the sandy soil and provide commercial timber, with Maritime pines making up 85% of the trees. The sand dunes are home to a variety of different plant life, including sand lilies, dune carnations, sand toadflax, rockroses, dune wallflowers and different species of samphire.

The presence of medium-sized mammals, including wild cats, marten, mink, roe deer, badgers and wild boar are most likely to be detected by the evidence they leave behind, such as the ploughing up of the forest floor by the nocturnal snuffling of wild boar.

BRITTANY

Cycling the pavé into Saint-Pol-de-Léon (Stage 1)

Roscoff
SAINT-MALO
BREST
Carhaix-
Plouguer
Mûr-de-Bretagne
RENNES
QUIMPER
Josselin
Redon
Nort-sur-Erdre
NANTES
N
0
25
50
km

STAGE 1

Roscoff to Carhaix-Plouguer

Start	Roscoff, tourist information office
Finish	Carhaix-Plouguer, steam locomotive memorial
Time	6hr 30min
Distance	79.9km
Ascent	790m
Descent	660m
Refreshments en route	Saint-Pol-de-Léon, Morlaix and Locmaria-Berrian
Accommodation en route	Saint-Pol-de-Léon and Morlaix

This relatively hilly stage, initially along undulating lanes surrounded by farmland and then through a river valley, leads to the historic medieval town of Morlaix, ideally located for a lunch stop. A long, gentle climb along a disused railway, through woodland and an agricultural landscape, leads to the market town of Carhaix-Plouguer.

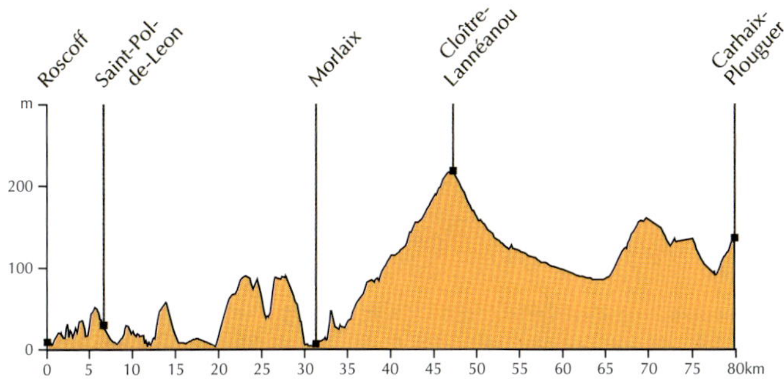

La Vélodyssée begins in the port town of Roscoff. Some may start their journey at either the station or the ferry port, but the La Vélodyssée 'Km 0' sign is located outside the tourist office, looking north across the sea from Quai d'Auxerre, providing an ideal opportunity for those who want a photographic record of the start of their Vélodyssée.

The 'Km 0' sign in front of the Roscoff tourist office

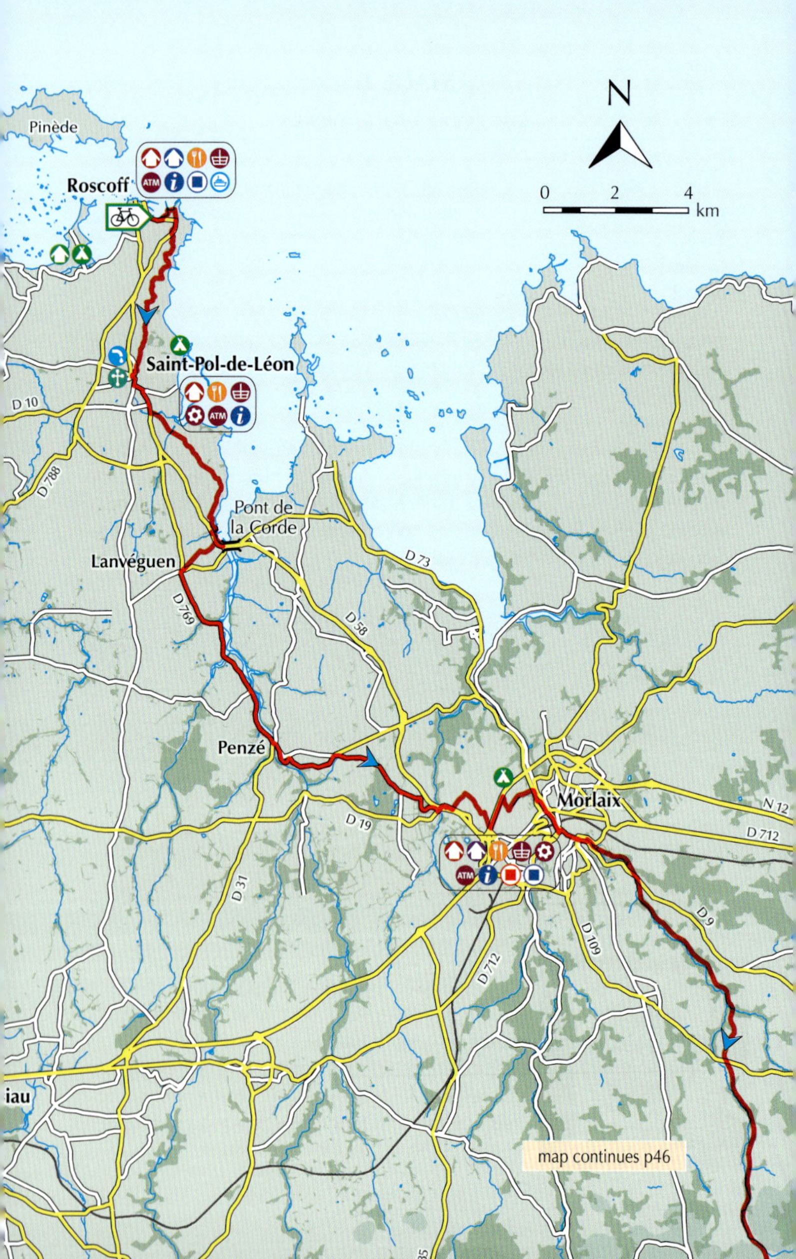
N
0
2
4
km
Pinède
Roscoff
Saint-Pol-de-Léon
D 10
D 788
Pont de
la Corde
Lanvéguen
D 769
D 73
D 58
Penzé
Morlaix
N 12
D 712
D 19
D 31
D 9
D 109
D 712
iau
ATM
map continues p46

Looking west across Roscoff harbour from Rue Jeanne d'Arc

Those close to retirement age, or beyond, may remember the **Onion Johnnies**. They travelled the south of England, often by bike, selling onions grown in Roscoff. Early salesmen began crossing the Channel once trade between England and France resumed in 1815. The cliché of cycling Frenchmen wearing stripy shirts and berets, festooned with strings of onions around their necks, has survived long after the practice was overtaken by modern vegetable sales and distribution methods. The Roscoff Onion now has appellation d'origine contrôlée status and is commemorated in La Maison des Johnnies et de l'Oignon de Roscoff museum.

From the tourist information office, head east along Quai d'Auxerre, which soon becomes Rue Jeanne d'Arc, for 350m to a triangular junction with Rue de Plymouth. Bear left to continue on Rue Jeanne d'Arc, and then straight ahead onto Rue Captain Coadou, following the eastern shore of the bay before rejoining Rue Jeanne d'Arc. After 350m, at the end of the eastern harbour wall, bear right onto Boulevard Sainte-Barbe, which runs beside a north-facing beach. After 200m, at the car park for the Chapelle Sainte-Barbe, turn right onto Rue de Great Torrington.

After 300m, bear right onto Rue Joseph le Mat, then bear left after 100m, back to meet the main road next to an old railway line. Turn right then immediately left, crossing both the road and the railway line, to continue in the same direction, using a track on the opposite side of the railway. Follow the track for 250m to the T-junction with Rue de Keraison. Turn left and follow the road for 350m, passing a tunnel under the railway that leads to the botanical gardens, to a T-junction by a tunnel that leads to the sandy Plage du Traon Erc'h.

Turn right, then at the crossroads after 200m, turn left to follow the lane for 200m, and then bear left onto Pors ar Bascon, crossing the bridge over the old railway line. After 550m, at the T-junction, turn right and follow the lane for 750m until it meets Rue de Kerfissiec. Follow this lane for 300m to a staggered crossroads, turn left and follow the lane for 2km until it meets the D769 at a T-junction. Turn left and follow the partially cobbled (pavé) street for 300m into **Saint-Pol-de-Léon** (**6.4km, 30min**). Continue around the cathedral, leaving the town centre on the Rue du Général Lerclerc, to arrive at the road junction by the imposing Chapelle Notre-Dame du Kreisker.

Turn left in front of the church and follow Rue Verderel for 300m to the roundabout by the cemetery gates. Bear right onto Rue de Morlaix then, after 600m, turn left onto Route de Trégondern. Follow the quiet lane for 4km, through fields of artichokes overlooking the sea, to the hamlet of Saint-Nep. Before reaching the busy D58, turn left onto a lane that soon becomes a track and then a road again to arrive at the riverbank after 400m. Turn right and follow the track and lane, which briefly runs alongside the D58, before arriving at the **Pont de la Corde** (**12.5km, 1hr**), which carries the D58 across the river Penzé.

Signs direct you almost back on yourself, along the side of the D58 for 200m, to where there is a recommended crossing place. Visibility of fast-moving traffic coming from your left is still not perfect, so considerable care is needed. Once across the D58, follow the quiet lane for 500m to a crossroads by a single dwelling. Turn left and follow the very straight road for 700m to the village of **Lanvéguen**. Just after the disused level crossing, turn left onto Route de Milinou. Follow the road down the hill and then along the riverside until you reach the bridge over the river in the village of **Penzé** (**19.6km, 1hr 35min**).

Continue along the D769 for 2.3km until you reach a crossroads with five ways. Turn right and follow the lane for 2km to a T-junction. Turn right and continue for 1km to another T-junction, then turn right again to reach a roundabout after 800m. Turn left, cross over the D58 dual carriageway and at the next roundabout, continue straight ahead. After 200m turn left and head up the hill for 600m, then turn right onto a track. Follow the track for 800m until, after a sharp left turn, it rejoins the road. Turn right and continue for 400m to a pedestrian crossing by a hotel. Take the path that leads to the left from the crossing and over a footbridge.

Descend from the footbridge and then turn left onto the lane that runs parallel to the busy N12. Follow this lane and path for 750m, then turn right onto Route de Kerserho. Follow the road straight across at the first roundabout, then at the second, after 300m, turn left onto a cycle lane that runs beside Rue de Saint Germain. After 800m, turn right onto Quai de Léon and follow this for 1.2km, beneath the towering viaduct, to the Place des Otages in front of the town hall in the centre of **Morlaix** (**31.4km, 2hr 35min**).

MORLAIX

Morlaix, a thriving historic town, is dominated by the impressive viaduct that carries the TGV line on its route from Paris to Brest. The town is well placed on this stage for a lunch stop, with a good range of shops and places to eat. It is also a popular stopover for those looking for a shorter first stage. From almost anywhere in the town, as you walk through the narrow, cobbled streets that weave between half-timbered buildings and pavement cafés, you can see the viaduct. Completed in 1863, it is 292m long, 58m high and built from 65,000m^3 of stone. It is possible to walk across the viaduct on the first level, which provides an excellent view of the town and an intriguing, much-photographed perspective, looking along the walkway between the arches.

Between Morlaix and the end of the stage there are no shops along the route, very few places to eat and few opportunities to refill water bottles. Leave the town centre along the Place des Otages, with the viaduct behind you, keeping the ornate bandstand and Hôtel de Ville (town hall) on your left. At the traffic lights, turn left onto Rue Carnot then right, signposted Callac, onto the Rue d'Aiguillon. After 200m, bear left onto Rue de Paris. Pass a bike shop on your right and continue for 300m to a roundabout.

View of the viaduct and St-Mélaine church from Morlaix's ancient streets

Go straight across onto Rue de Callac and then after 300m, at the mini roundabout painted on the road, turn left onto Place du Pouliet. Cross the river Jarlot and turn right. After passing a car park on your right, bear right onto Rue du Moulin de la Chèvre. Follow this road for 400m until it drops away to the right and there are staggered wooden barriers across a track on your left. Turn left onto the track and then, after 200m, bear right onto the old railway.

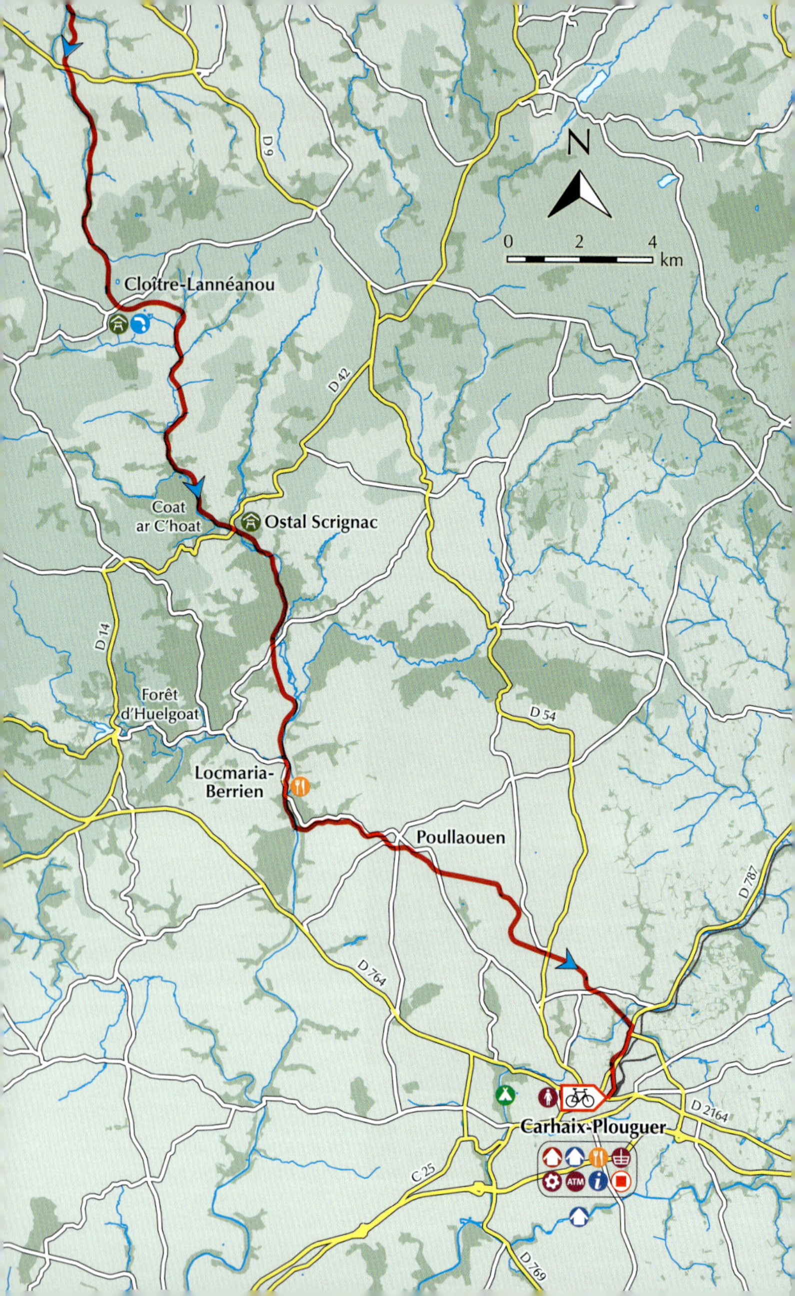

N
0
2
4
km
D 9
Cloître-Lannéanou
D 42
Coat
ar C'hoat
Ostal Scrignac
D 14
Forêt
d'Huelgoat
D 54
Locmaria-
Berrien
Poullaouen
D 787
D 764
Carhaix-Plouguer
D 2164
C 25
ATM
D 769

Picnic site at a former station near Scrignac

Voie Verte No. 7 now heads through open fields and woodland, often with the trees on each side meeting to form a canopy above the foxglove-lined trail. You climb gently but continuously for the next 14.2km until you arrive at the derelict station building of **Cloître-Lannéanou** (**47.2km, 3hr 55min**). There are picnic tables here and a drinking tap. After crossing the road, the route now starts to descend before arriving at **Ostal Scrignac**, another former station building, after 9.2km (**56.4km, 4hr 40min**). There are picnic tables here too.

The route continues to descend for a further 7.8km to reach the old station at **Locmaria-Berrien** (**64.2km, 5hr 15min**). There is a choice of places to eat here, including a quirky Cambodian restaurant in the station building. After 4.5km of gentle climbing, the route arrives at a cemetery on the outskirts of the small town of **Poullaouen** (**68.6km, 5hr 40min**).

Continue along the voie verte for 9km of gentle descent until, shortly after crossing the river L'Hyères, you arrive at the D787. Turn right and follow the cycle

The restored Mallet type steam locomotive marking the end of Stage 1

track beside the road, continuing straight across at the roundabout for 1.5km to a large roundabout next to a supermarket. Cross the roundabout onto Rue Salvador Allende and follow the road for 1km to the train station at **Carhaix-Plouguer** and the end of the stage (**79.9km, 6hr 30min**).

CARHAIX-PLOUGUER

Situated on a plateau 140m above sea level, the town of Carhaix was once a significant transport hub, lying at the junction of train lines and the Nantes–Brest canal. Today the town hosts one of the biggest music festivals in France, the Vieilles Charrues Festival, with up to 200,000 people attending.

Carhaix also has a penchant for celebrating its former citizens with statues; these include a footballer, local sisters who were agricultural workers and helped to maintain the Breton language, legendary Breton cyclists, a train driver and a policeman. Among the statues of cyclists, those with an interest in the history of Grand tour racing will recognise Lucian Mazan (Petit-Breton), who took up cycling after he won a bike in a lottery. He became the first cyclist to win the Tour de France twice but was tragically killed in World War 1. Another cycling legend, Bernard Hinault, leads the pack of statues. Hinault won the Tour de France five times in the 70s and 80s.

STAGE 2

Carhaix-Plouguer to Mûr-de-Bretagne

Start	Carhaix-Plouguer, steam locomotive memorial
Finish	Mûr-de-Bretagne, former railway station
Time	3hr 45min
Distance	64.3km
Ascent	360m
Descent	350m
Refreshments en route	Gouarec and L'Abbaye de Bon-Repos
Accommodation en route	Multiple locations along the route

After a short descent on mostly quiet lanes and tracks from the centre of Carhaix, you arrive at the Nantes–Brest canal. Much of the stage now follows the canal towpath through woodland and rural landscapes, passing the pretty village of Gouarec and the ancient ruined abbey at Bon-Repos, both well suited to a lunch stop, before continuing along a disused railway track to Mûr-de-Bretagne.

From the roundabout by the locomotive memorial, head south along Impasse du Lavoir. At the end of the lane continue straight ahead onto a track and then briefly along Chemin de la Salette before another signed track leads off to the left. Follow this track to arrive at Boulouard Jean Moulin, 600m after leaving the locomotive.

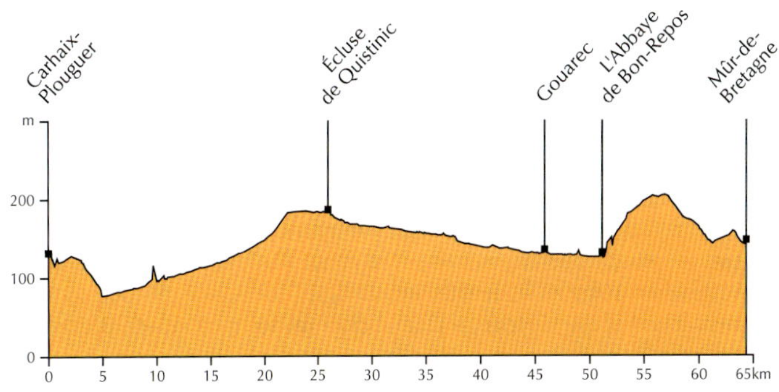

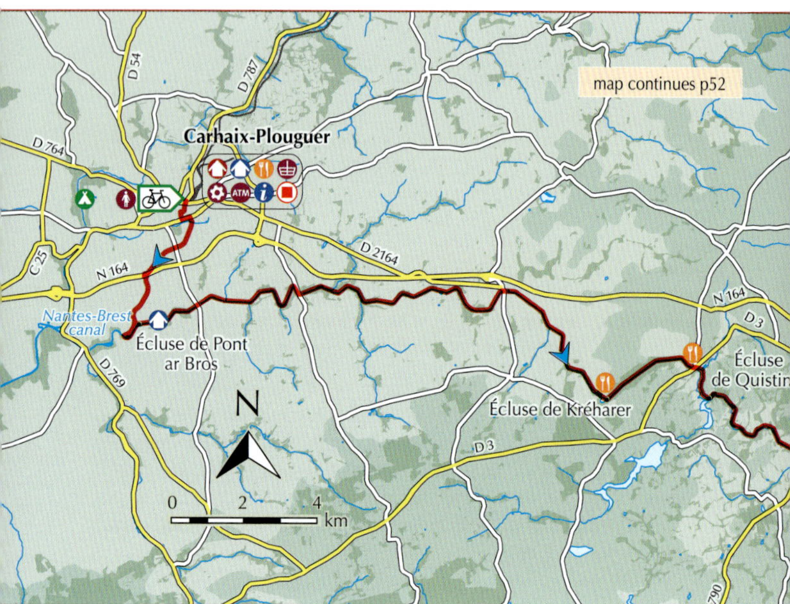

Turn left and follow the road for 200m to a signposted track on the right, opposite a car showroom. Follow this track down the hill for 2.2km until it meets Route de Kergaled, next to the N164. Head under the bridge and then turn immediately left. Follow the track round to the right and continue down the hill for 2km until you meet the **Nantes–Brest canal** (**5km, 15min**).

Turn left under the bridge and follow the canal east. The Nantes–Brest canal will now be your companion for most of the journey to Nantes.

THE NANTES–BREST CANAL

When the canal was originally built, it had 238 locks and ran for 360km. It was conceived in 1783 to provide an inland route between France's two largest Atlantic military ports when Brest was blockaded by the British fleet, eventually opening in 1842. The canal was closed to navigation in 1920, when 10km of its length, including 17 locks, was flooded for the construction of the Guerlédan Dam, below the town of Mûr-de-Bretagne.

Nantes–Brest canal towpath between Gouarec and Bon-Repos

The absence of the 26m-long barges, which could carry up to 140 tonnes, led to sections silting up. Only limited sections are now navigable, but the restoration of the towpath for walking and cycling and the creation of La Vélodyssée have resulted in a welcome increase in tourism in the area, using a transport link that was built more than two centuries ago.

Shortly after joining the canal, you pass **Écluse de Pont ar Bros**. Each of the écluses (locks) is given a number, which is usually found on a sign next to the lock – for example, Écluse de Pont ar Bros is No. 200.

Continue along the canal towpath as it climbs gently for 17km, passing 40 locks, until you reach the large basin at **Écluse de Kréharer** (No. 160) (**22km, 1hr 15min**), where there is a café. Continuing along the towpath, you enter the section of the canal called the Glomel Trench. As this is the highest part of the canal, the water has been flowing towards you up to this point. After a further 4.2km of towpath, passing a café at Pont ar Len, you arrive at **Écluse de Quistinic** (No. 159)

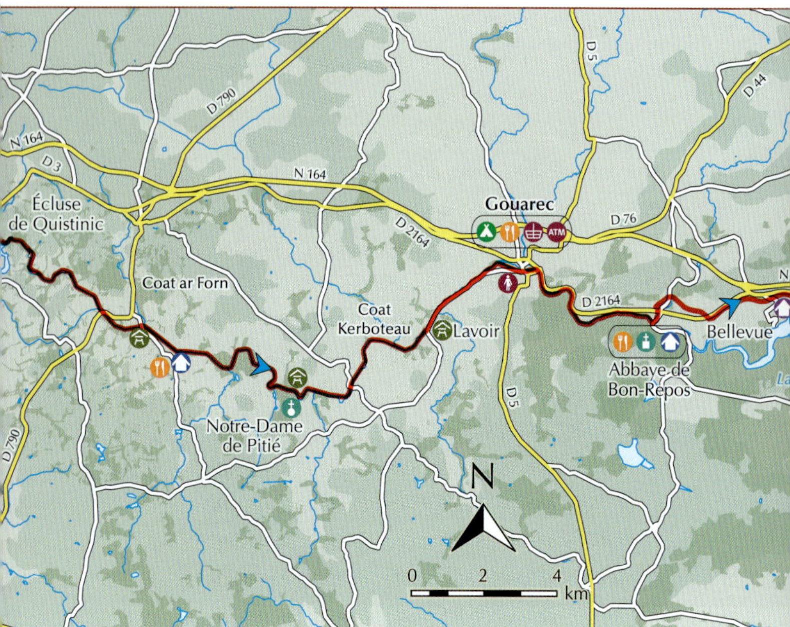

(**26.2km, 1hr 30min**), and the water now starts to flow in the same direction as you are cycling.

After you have cycled 11.5km of beautiful towpath, passing picnic tables at Écluse de Kerjégu (No. 151) and a crêperie at Écluse de Bonen (No. 150), the canal widens on a bend, revealing the picturesque chapel of **Notre-Dame de Pitié** on the far bank of the canal (**37.7km, 2hr 10min**). It can be viewed from the covered picnic table next to the trail.

After 4.9km, at Écluse de Plélauff (No. 142), the route crosses over the canal and there is a picnic site next to an old lavoir (public laundry). Continuing for 3.4km, you arrive at the pretty village of **Gouarec** (**46km, 2hr 40min**), where there is a campsite adjacent to the canal and a café that few cyclists seem able to pass without stopping. Crossing the bridge in front of the café leads into the centre of the village in 250m, which offers a shop, bakery, places to eat and an ancient covered market square.

Continue along the canal, which is now the river Blavet, for 5km to the imposing ruined **Abbaye de Bon-Repos** (**51km, 3hr**).

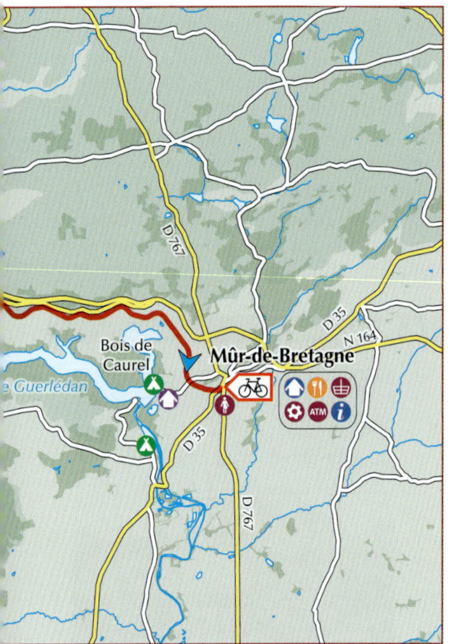

The ancient covered market hall in Gouarec

The charismatic **Abbaye de Bon-Repos** stands on the north bank of the river, casting its dramatic reflection onto the water. It was founded in 1184 after Viscount Alain III of Rohan claimed to have been visited by the Virgin Mary in a dream; he then gave the site to the Cistercian monks to build the abbey. It thrived for more than 200 years, profiting from its rich agricultural land and woodland, before it began to slip into decline. In the 17th century, it was remodelled and auctioned off for the benefit of the nation after the revolution in 1789. Two hundred years of structural decline followed before partial renovations were started in the 1990s. It now hosts art exhibitions and tours and has a restaurant, café and several gîtes on site.

Cross the bridge towards the abbey. Once over the bridge, a large sign offers the option of two routes: one described as difficile (difficult) turns right and follows the north bank until it reaches Écluse des Forges (No. 137); it then climbs steeply up the hill to Bellevue. La Vélodyssée takes the second option, labelled facile (easy), which continues straight ahead for 150m after the bridge then turns left onto a track towards the abbey car park, just after the first entrance to the abbey on your right.

Cross the D2164, take the lane in front of you to the left of the cottages and follow this for 200m. After a bend to the left, take the signposted track on your right. Follow the track along the former railway for 1.7km, passing over a viaduct, until it meets the D2164 again. Go straight across and then turn left onto a short section of lane at **Bellevue** before bearing left to rejoin the cycle track.

Follow the track for 10.5km until it ends at Rue de la Gare in **Mûr-de-Bretagne**. Turn left, then after 200m, turn left again into the car park at the old station building (**64.3km, 3hr 45min**).

MÛR-DE-BRETAGNE

Mûr-de-Bretagne, or Guerlédan in Breton, exhibits a quiet civic pride. It has hosted the finish of a stage of the Tour de France on four occasions, between 2011 and 2025, which it commemorates with the yellow statue of a cyclist displayed in front of the town hall. There are places to stay, eat and shop, including a popular bakery. Next to the Église Sainte-Pierre de Guerlédan, which sports impressive gargoyles, there is a small town square. Good campsites are located by the shores of the lake a short way along the next stage of the route at Lac de Guerlédan, where there is also a small beach.

Mûr-de-Bretagne celebrating its involvement with the Tour de France

STAGE 3

Mûr-de-Bretagne to Josselin

Start	Mûr-de-Bretagne, former railway station
Finish	Josselin, Château de Josselin
Time	3hr 45min
Distance	72km
Ascent	220m
Descent	330m
Refreshments en route	Pontivy and Rohan
Accommodation en route	Pontivy and Rohan

The stage descends along quiet lanes and cycle tracks to Lac de Guerlédan to rejoin the Nantes–Brest canal. You then follow the towpath through the historic canal-side towns of Rohan and Pontivy, both worth exploring, before finishing the stage beneath the towering walls of the Château de Josselin.

Leaving Mûr-de-Bretagne, you initially retrace your route from Stage 2, first along Rue de la Gare and then for 500m along the cycle track towards Gouarec. At a well-signposted junction, bear left, following the sign to Canal de Nantes–Brest.

Continue along the track and then road, heading down the hill. Keep right at the forked junction after 700m, then arrive at Écluse de Guerlédan (No. 119) (**3km, 10min**) and the impressive dam and **Lac de Guerlédan**.

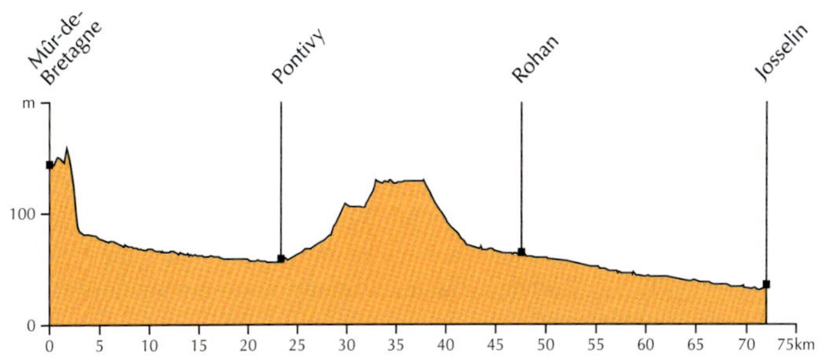

A track junction near the start of Stage 3

Lac de Guerlédan, the largest artificial lake in Brittany, was created by the construction of the Barrage de Guerlédan. The dam was built between 1923 and 1930 to generate hydroelectricity. Seventeen locks on the Nantes–Brest canal were submerged during the creation of the lake, although they have periodically made ghostly appearances when the lake has been drained to inspect the hydroelectric systems. This happened regularly from the 1950s, but when it was most recently drained, in 2015, new maintenance access was installed to allow it to be inspected without draining the lake.

Turn left onto the towpath beside the canal, which is now navigable. Continue for 16.8km, passing a picnic table at Écluse de Boloré (No. 114), to Écluse de Guernal (No. 109), where there is an imposing derelict mill on the far bank. Continue for 3.6km to the historic town of **Pontivy** (**23.4km, 1hr 15min**). The town is worth taking the time to explore, with plenty of places to eat, drink and stock up on supplies.

PONTIVY

This fascinating historic town has suffered numerous identity crises over its 1400-year history. The town was founded in the seventh century by a monk called Ivy, who built the bridge which was then named after him, 'Pont-Ivy', and the town was named after the bridge. It remained a small quiet town until the 15th century, when the wealthy Rohan family built the moated Château des Rohan, leading to the growth of the medieval town around it.

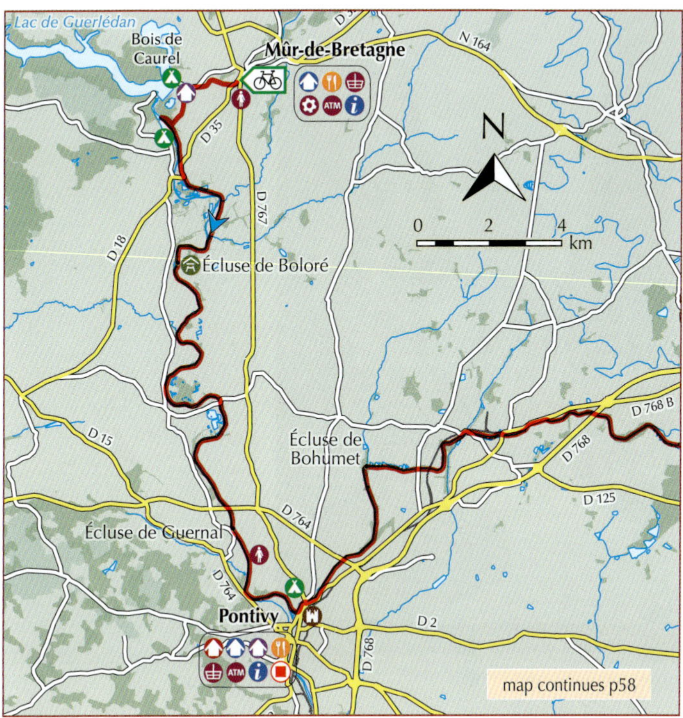

Pontivy saw another boost to its prosperity in the 18th century, with the opening of two canals, the Nantes–Brest canal and the Canal du Blavet, which heads south-west from Pontivy to the major Atlantic port of Lorient. These two building booms created a town of two halves: a medieval quarter centred around the castle, with narrow streets and half-timbered buildings, and an 18th-century quarter with wide straight boulevards and elegant town houses. As a result of these developments, the town struggled to settle on its name. Known as Pontivy from its founding until 1804, it was then renamed Napoléonville in honour of Napoleon Bonaparte. After his downfall it was rechristened Pontivy and then Bourbonville, following the restoration of the monarchy. It became Napoléonville again when Napoleon III was crowned emperor before returning to Pontivy for a third time.

Half-timbered buildings in the centre of Pontivy

As you leave Pontivy, make sure you are following the canal towpath, which heads north-east, signposted with La Vélodyssée logoed signs to Rohan and Josselin, and with the water flowing towards you. (With the canal having made navigation so straightforward for most of the route from Carhaix, you would be forgiven for mistakenly setting off on the Blavet Canal towpath, which heads south-west towards Lorient and has V6 logoed signs).

From the Écluse du Ponteau (No. 107), follow the towpath for 4.6km to **Écluse de Bohumet** (No. 98), where the canal bends to the right and an impressive series of locks, each with a large lagoon next to it, leads after 5km to Écluse de Keroret (No. 79) (**33km, 1hr 45min**). Since you left Pontivy, 29 locks have lifted the canal by 75m. There are now no locks for the next 5km, until you reach Écluse de Bel Air (No. 78). The canal now gently descends for the next 9.8km to the town of **Rohan** (**47.8km, 2hr 30min**).

Rohan is a pleasant town, although it lacks the dramatic historical architecture of its canal-side neighbours of Pontivy and Josselin. It is ideally placed for a

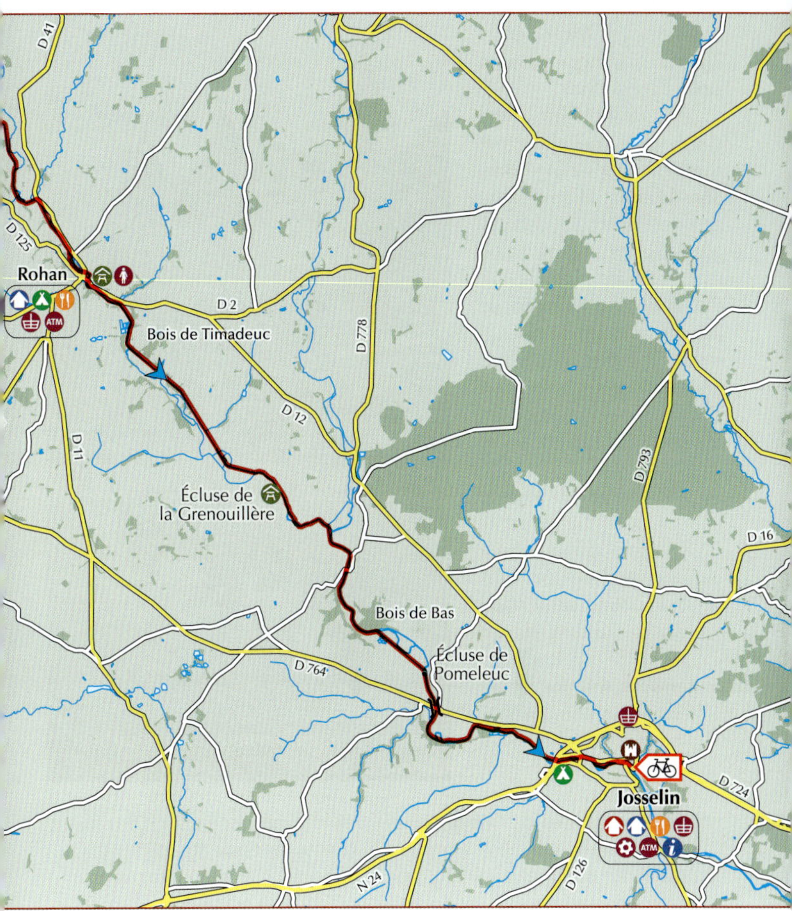

lunch break, with a supermarket and restaurants in the town and picnic tables adjacent to the canal.

Follow the towpath for 8.3km to **Écluse de la Grenouillère** (No. 46), where there is a Place des Cyclistes: a picnic site adjacent to the canal with tables and a barbecue. Continue for 7.8km **to Écluse de Pomeleuc** (No. 40) (**63.9km, 3hr 20min**), where the canal merges with the Oust river. After another 1km, the route crosses over the river at Bocneuf and then continues along the east bank.

The final 7.3km of the stage takes you along the riverbank to Josselin (**72km, 3hr 45min**). Historically, architecturally and photogenically, the stage has saved its best till last. The view of the imposing **Château de Josselin** reflected on the surface of the river over which it towers is probably the most photographed location on this section of La Vélodyssée.

Château de Josselin reflected in the canal at the end of Stage 3

The **Château de Josselin** is a castle straight out of children's drawings, with its conical-roofed circular towers and solid stone walls. Building started in 1173 and has been ongoing for most of the following 850 years as the fortunes of its owners fluctuated, with parts being destroyed and then rebuilt. It has been in the ownership of the Rohan family for the last 500 years and continues to be their family home. Parts of the castle are open to the public, displaying fine furnishings acquired from the 17th to the 19th century. Behind the castle lies the town of equal antiquity, with houses dating back to 1538. Of all the historic towns on this part of the route, Josselin is the easiest place in which to imagine you have been whisked back to the medieval period. It is well supplied with places to eat to suit all budgets, and there is a similar range of accommodation on offer.

STAGE 4

Josselin to Redon

Start	Josselin, Château de Josselin
Finish	Redon, Écluse des Bateliers
Time	3hr 50min
Distance	62.8km
Ascent	180m
Descent	210m
Refreshments en route	Montertelot, Le Roc-Saint-André, Malestroit, Saint-Congard, Saint-Martin-sur-Oust, Le Pont d'Oust and Painfaut
Accommodation en route	Malestroit, Saint-Congard, Saint-Martin-sur-Oust, Le Pont d'Oust and Painfaut

From Josselin, you continue south-east along the Nantes–Brest canal, passing through the pretty medieval town of Malestroit, with its plentiful supply of shops and pavement cafés making it an ideal lunch stop, before finishing the stage at the ancient port of Redon. It's a stage of flat, tranquil cycling with a medieval theme.

From the Château de Josselin, head south-east along the Nantes–Brest canal for 8km to where a small path is signposted off to the left to the Fontaine Saint-Bertin. The drinking water fountain was built in 1651 to rid the parish of the plague. After a further 700m, the canal broadens into a basin at Écluse de Guillac (No. 31), where there are picnic tables beside the canal.

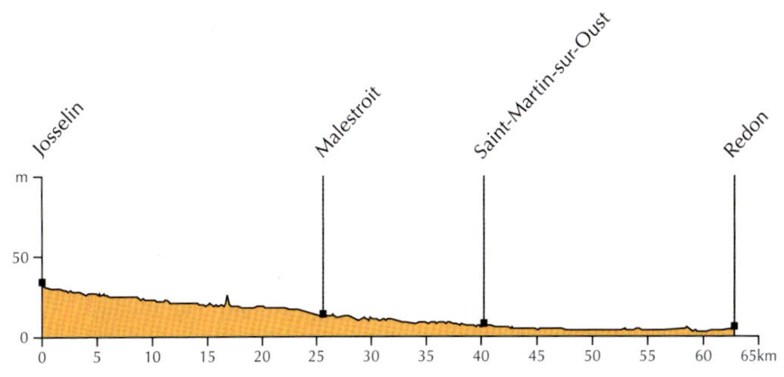

The Pont Neuf at Malestroit

Continuing along the canal for 4km, you pass a pop-up café and crêperie as you cross the D174 at L'Herbinaye, and a watermill with a waterwheel at Écluse de Blon (No. 30), before arriving under the former railway bridge that now carries the Voie Vert No. 3 north-eastwards to Saint-Malo. After a further 1.3km, you arrive at the pretty canal-side village of **Montertelot** (**14km, 50min**). This is a popular stopping place for cyclists, walkers, boat cruisers and motorists. It is generously supplied with picnic tables around the lock-keeper's cottage and the church and offers a bar and a restaurant with pavement tables.

After a further 3km, passing the impressive Château de Crévy, and underneath another iron bridge of the Voie Verte No. 3 (V3), you arrive at **Le Roc-Saint-André** (**16.9km, 1hr**), where the route crosses from the east to the west bank of the river. The village offers places to eat and a canal-side campsite. Continuing for 5.5km, having passed under the V3 for the third and final time, and the less attractive road bridge of the busy N166, the Nantes–Brest canal temporarily parts company with the river Oust at Écluse de la Née Garde (No. 27). You now follow an arrow-straight route along the canal towpath for 3km to the well-preserved medieval town of **Malestroit** (**25.5km, 1hr 35min**).

MALESTROIT

Malestroit has a beautiful medieval centre, with pavement cafés in the pedestrianised square by the church, a supermarket and a bakery. It has half-timbered buildings and a mixture of narrow streets and open squares with interesting shops. In 1343, representatives of Philip VI of France and Edward III of England signed the Truce of Malestroit at the Chapelle de la Madeleine.

Situated roughly halfway between Josselin and Redon, Malestroit is, unsurprisingly, a popular lunch stop on this stage. For those wishing to spend more time completing La Vélodyssée, there is a range of accommodation, including a popular campsite next to the canal, a short walk from the town.

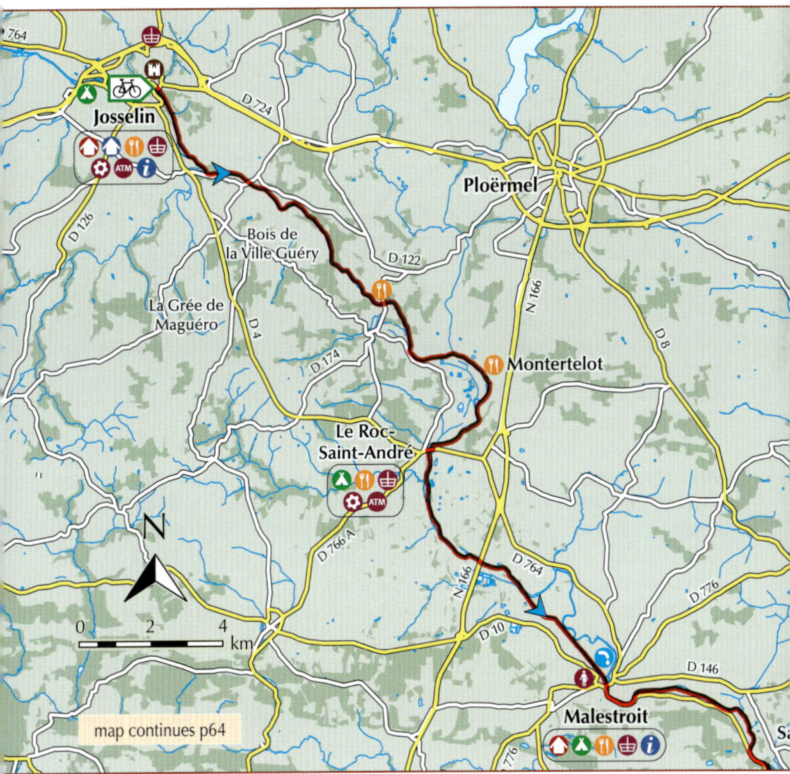

Leaving Malestroit, the canal rejoins the river and meanders its way through a rural landscape, with beautiful vistas of the foliage reflecting in the water around every bend, and it is punctuated by well-maintained locks and cottages, making this stretch of the route a memorable ride.

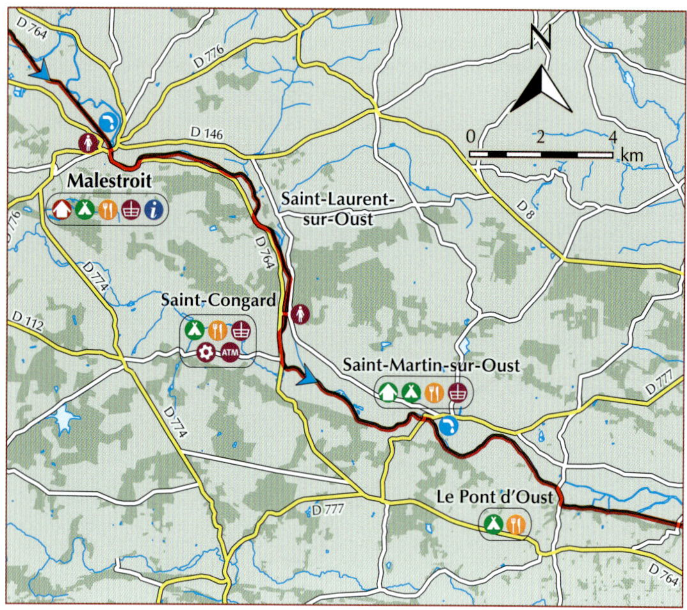

After 5.6km, you pass under the elegant foot bridge at **Saint-Laurent-sur-Oust**, and in a further 2.9km, there is a canal-side campsite at **Saint-Congard** (**34.1km, 2hr 5min**). Continue for 6.3km to **Saint-Martin-sur-Oust** (**40.3km, 2hr 30min**). If you cross over the bridge, the village offers a choice of accommodation, including a municipal campsite next to the canal, as well as places to eat and covered picnic tables overlooking the water.

Continue along the south bank of the canal for 5.3km to **Le Pont d'Oust**, where there is a canal-side campsite and public swimming pool. After 2.4km, at Écluse de Limur (No. 20), the canal again parts ways with the Oust and follows a straight course for 4.5km before rejoining the river at Écluse de la Maclais (No. 19). A further 800m brings you to L'Île-aux-Pies, near the village of **Painfaut** (**53.3km, 3hr 15min**), where there are two campsites, a café and a range of

Looking across the river to the route from the falaises de L'île aux Pies at Painfaut

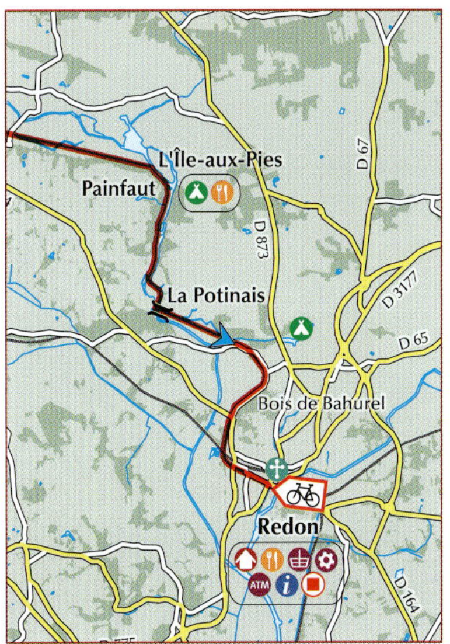

outdoor activities available. These include a high-ropes course, canoe hire and, on the far side of the river, a crag that is popular with both experienced climbers and beginners' groups. On a summer's day, the valley is filled with the excited sounds of adventures unfolding on the trail, water and crag.

Continuing for 2.9km along the bank of the river, you reach **La Potinais**, where the river Oust and the Nantes–Brest canal part ways for the last time. After the picnic bench and car park, turn left over the bridge and follow the canal towpath, initially along a straight section, followed by some sweeping bends, for 6.7km to Écluse des Bateliers in **Redon** (**62.8km, 3hr 50min**). Here the Nantes–Brest canal meets the river Vilaine.

REDON

Compared with its well-preserved medieval neighbours upstream, Redon has a 20th-century feel to it, but you only need to scratch a little at the surface for it to reveal its historical delights. The Abbatiale Saint-Sauveure church in the centre of town is a mixture of Roman and Gothic styles of architecture. It has medieval frescoes and 18th-century cloisters formed from arcades surrounding peaceful gardens. The cobbled Grand Rue is lined with a mixture of half-timbered and stone buildings, with the oldest, the Hôtel des Monnaies, dating back to 1420. It was in Redon, in 1489, that Henry VII of England signed the Treaty of Redon in which he agreed to send 6000 English troops in an unsuccessful attempt to prevent Brittany becoming part of France.

Along the waterfront on the Quai Saint-Jacques, the elegant 18th-century merchants' and shipowners' houses tell of the time when trade on the canal brought prosperity to the town. Pleasure cruisers on the river and cyclists on La Vélodyssée are now helping to create a new renaissance for the town.

L'Abbaye Saint-Sauveur at Redon

STAGE 5

Redon to Nort-sur-Erdre

Start	Redon, Écluse des Bateliers
Finish	Nort-sur-Erdre, tourist information office, Quai Saint-Georges
Time	4hr 25min
Distance	72.5km
Ascent	110m
Descent	110m
Refreshments en route	Guenrouet and Blain
Accommodation en route	Guenrouet and Blain

This flat stage is divided by two towns into roughly three equal parts. From Redon the route follows the canal towpath to the village of Guenrouet, then it takes a meandering course as the canal uses the river L'Isac to the historic town of Blain, with its impressive castle. After Blain, more canal-side cycling follows, and then quiet lanes and a cycleway lead into the town of Nort-sur-Erdre.

From the Écluse des Bateliers, head south-east, keeping the canal on your left, along Quai Amiral de la Grandière, passing underneath the low cast-iron bridge, which carries the Grande Rue over the Écluse de Redon Oust (No. 19). Continue along Quai Amiral de la Grandière for a short distance until you meet the river Vilaine at the T-junction with Quai Duguay-Trouin. The canal continues ahead on the other side of La Vilaine.

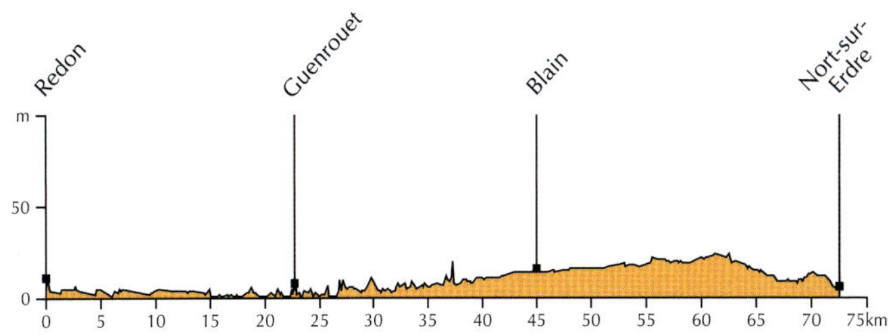

To get to that point by bike, turn left to pass over the canal, then take your first right onto the bridge that carries the D775 over La Vilaine. Once over the river, turn immediately right, go through the car park and cross back over the canal using the small bridge next to Écluse de la Digue (No. 18). Once over the canal, you rejoin the towpath by turning left onto Quai Georgette Beaudouin.

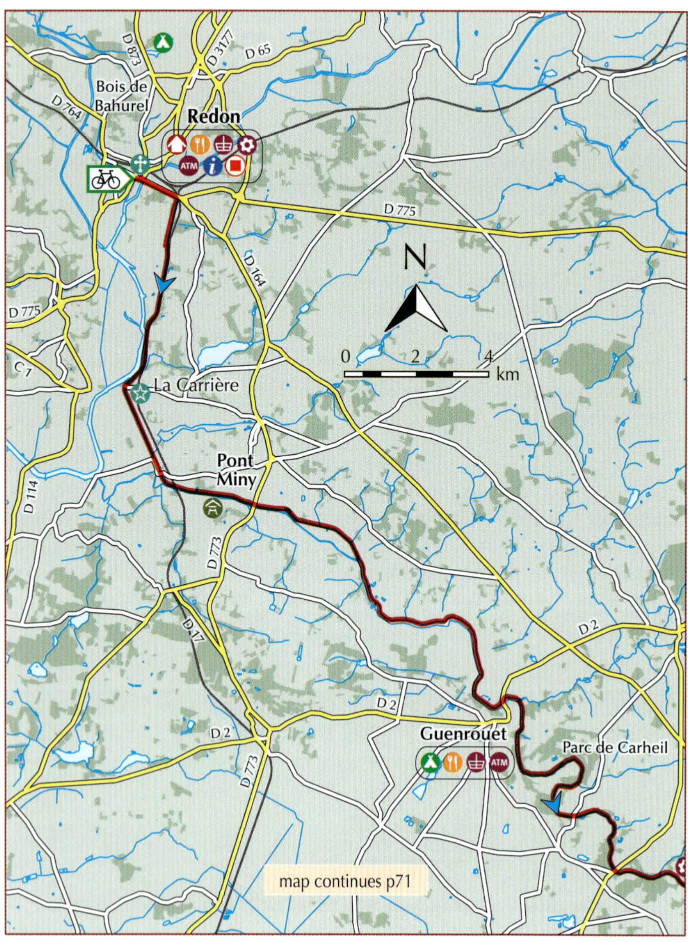

An excellent picnic site beside the canal at Pont Miny

Follow the southern towpath of the canal, initially south-east and then south, until after 2.7km the route crosses the canal via a small road bridge, from the west to the east bank. Continue along the canal for another 4.1km until you reach Écluse des Bellions (No. 17), the navigable junction of La Vilaine and the Nantes–Brest canal. An interesting art installation, La Carrière, has been created in an old quarry above the trail to provide an open-air performance space. Unless you are stopping for a break, or fancy a look at the river, don't let the generic cycle path signs tempt you across the bridge over the canal. La Vélodyssée continues along the towpath on the same bank as you arrived.

After 5.1km, you arrive at **Pont Miny**, where there are picnic tables beside the canal. After a short distance further along the towpath, you pass under the busy D773 and there then follows 10.8km of meandering canal-side cycling to the village of **Guenrouet** (**22.7km, 1hr 25min**). The town has places to buy food, eat – including a restaurant overlooking the canal – and a campsite. The village centre is a short climb up the hill.

The route continues along the same bank of the Nantes–Brest canal, which is now also the river L'Isac. It meanders 11km to Écluse de La Touche (No. 15), which has a small pop-up café popular with cyclists. Continue for 2.4km to Écluse de Barel (No. 14). Shortly after the lock, a drinking water tap is located beside the route, next to a picnic bench. After 9.1km, you pass under a disused cast-iron railway bridge, which spans the canal, and arrive in **Blain** (**45.2km, 2hr 45min**).

To the south of the canal is the Château de Blain, with an adjacent campsite and choice of gîtes. To the north of the river lies the town of Blain, which offers places to stay, shop and eat, including two on Quai Surcouf, with outside tables overlooking the canal.

Château de Blain, which is also known as Château de la Groulais, was originally built around 1108 by Alain IV, Duke of Brittany, as a defensive fort to guard the frontier against the invasion of Brittany by the Franks. The medieval castle – of which three towers, the entrance and some of the impressive walls

Château de Blain viewed from the route at Quai Surcou

remain – was constructed in the 13th century. In 1628 it was the home of Henri II, Duke of Rohan, who led the Protestant princes during the Wars of Religion, until it was partially destroyed on the orders of Cardinal Richelieu. It was rebuilt and extensively remodelled in the 16th century, creating the elegant chateau that can be seen today.

Continue along the north bank of the canal for 9.6km to Écluse de Remaudais (No. 8). At 800m after the lock, the route crosses from the north to the south bank of the canal. Then in 1.5km, the canal passes under the busy N137 and over the less busy D537. After a further 5.5km, cross the canal using the road bridge and continue east along the north bank for 2.2km to **Écluse de Cramezeul** (No. 6) (**64.8km, 4hr**). There is an inviting pop-up café next to the towpath, which proves very attractive to cyclists. Continue along the towpath for 2km and cross over the D164 at Écluse de la Rabinière (No. 4). After 1.2km, cross the D16 at the Pont du Plessis.

After a further 800m, it is time to temporarily leave the canal and take the cycleway that leads off the towpath to your left. The cycle route from here to Nort-sur-Erdre is well signed, with both pictures of cyclists painted on the road and green-and-white-cycle signposts. Continue 500m to a T-junction, turn left and follow the waymarked route through the hamlet of **Le Plessis-Pas-Brunet**, taking the right fork at the two Y-junctions. After 350m take the cycle route that is signed to your left.

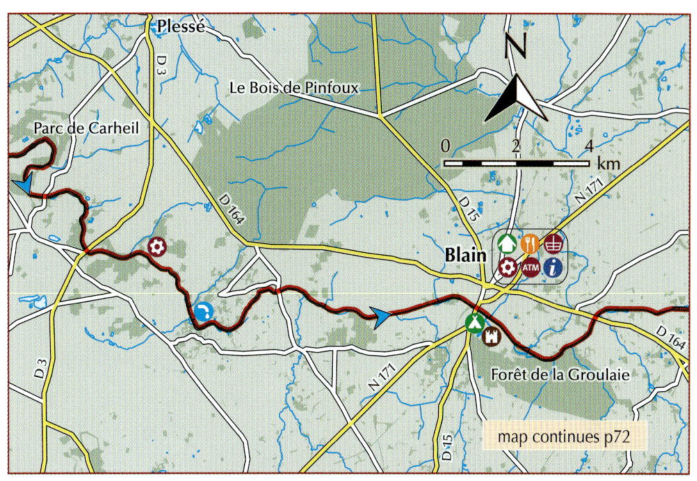

Pleasant riding along the canal towpath

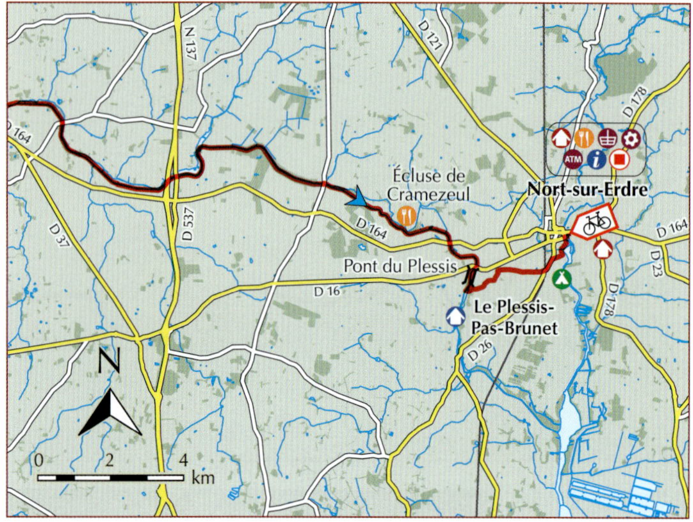

Follow the cycleway, initially car free, and then the quiet residential Rue des Frênes for 1.5km to the junction with Rue François Dupas. Go straight ahead at this junction, cross the level crossing and follow the road for 400m, passing the football ground on your right, then turn right onto Rue des Galopeurs. Follow this road for 600m as it first meets the Erdre river and then arrives at the marina. At the end of the marina, by the statue of Notre-Dame de Boulogne, turn right, cross a footbridge and arrive at the **Nort-sur-Erdre** tourist information office on Quai Saint-Georges (**72.5km, 4hr 30min**).

The town works hard to welcome holidaymakers, and its tourism is focused on the outdoors, with river cruises on the Erdre, and numerous parks criss-crossed with walking paths and waymarked cycle routes. There is a choice of campsites and other places to stay, as well as a plentiful supply of shops and places to eat.

The port at Nort-sur-Erdre

STAGE 6

Nort-sur-Erdre to Nantes

Start	Nort-sur-Erdre, tourist information office, Quai St Georges
Finish	Nantes, Passerelle Victor Schoelcher
Time	2hr 30min
Distance	38.7km
Ascent	200m
Descent	200m
Refreshments en route	Sucé-sur-Erdre
Accommodation en route	N/a

This shorter stage at the end of the Brittany section of the route gives you time to experience more of what Nantes has to offer. After following cycleways back to the Nantes–Brest canal from Nort-sur-Erdre, you head along the towpath for the final time before following quiet lanes to Sucé-sur-Erdre. As you continue along the Erdre valley, the landscape begins to change from rural to urban the closer you get to Nantes. Dedicated cycle lanes run alongside increasingly busy thoroughfares before leading you back to the river, which is followed to its confluence with the Loire in the centre of the thriving historic city of Nantes.

The first 3.7km of this stage is mostly reversing the end of Stage 5, back to the Nantes–Brest canal. From the tourist information office, cross the river Erdre via the footbridge and continue along Place du Bassin with the marina on your left.

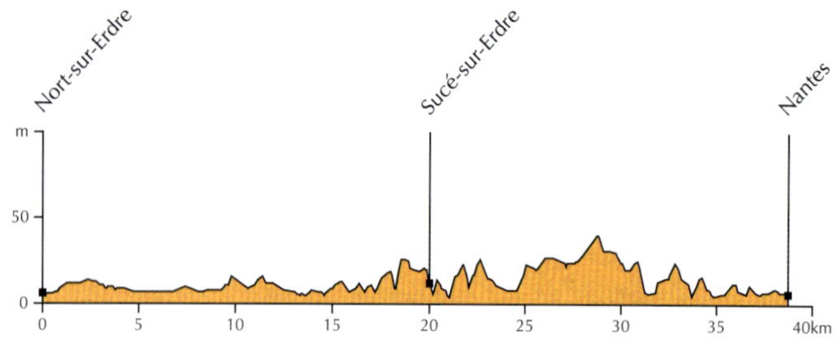

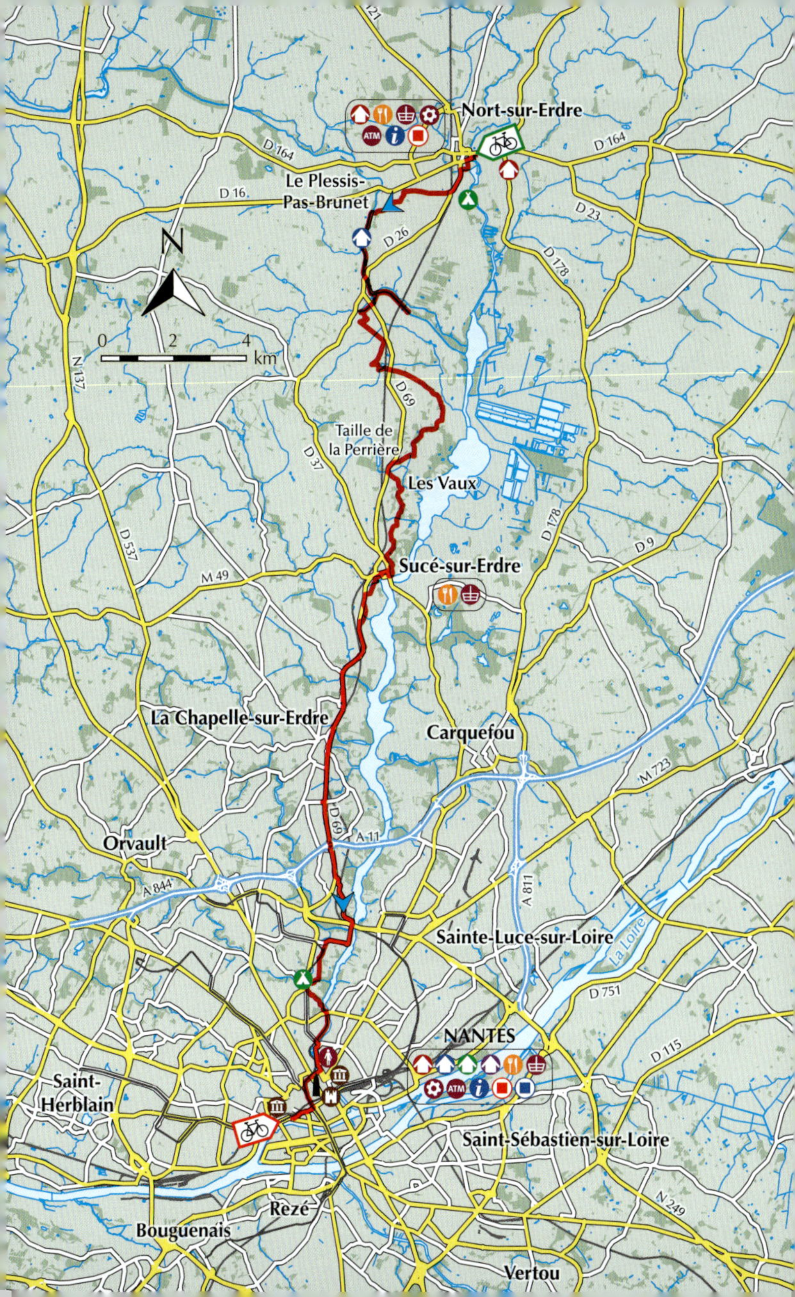

Nort-sur-Erdre
D 164
D 164
Le Plessis-
Pas-Brunet
D 16
D 26
D 23
D 178
N
0
2
4
km
N 137
D 69
Taille de
la Perrière
D 37
Les Vaux
D 178
D 537
D 9
M 49
Sucé-sur-Erdre
La Chapelle-sur-Erdre
Carquefou
M 723
D 69
A 11
Orvault
A 844
A 811
Sainte-Luce-sur-Loire
La Loire
D 751
NANTES
D 115
Saint-
Herblain
Saint-Sébastien-sur-Loire
N 249
Rezé
Bouguenais
Vertou

Waymarking on signs at the start of Stage 6

At the end of the marina, by the statue of Notre-Dame de Boulogne, continue straight ahead onto Boulevard Paul Doumer for 100m. Turn left and follow Rue des Écoles for 300m until a T-junction with Rue François Dupas. Turn left and follow the road for 800m, passing the football ground on your left, until you reach the level crossing.

Immediately over the railway line, take Rue des Frênes, which is straight ahead and signposted for La Vélodyssée. Follow this well-marked cycleway for 1.5km, which is initially a quiet residential road and then a car-free cycleway. At the end of the cycleway turn right through the hamlet of Le Plessis-Pas-Brunet. The route is now well waymarked, with both pictures of cyclists painted on the road and signposts to La Vélodyssée and the Nantes–Brest canal. Follow the signed route for 1km until you reach the canal (**3.7km, 15min**).

Turn left onto the canal towpath heading south. Pass the Écluse de la Tindière (No. 3), where the lock-keeper's cottage has been converted into a B&B, and cross over the **D26** and follow the towpath around a 90-degree bend. As the towpath crosses a sluice bridge, look across the canal and you will see a smaller canal joining the main waterway; the route will take you there in a few minutes. Continue under the railway until you arrive at a bridge, 3.6km after joining the canal. This is where the route stops following the Nantes–Brest canal, which has been your companion since Carhaix-Plouguer on Stage 2. The canal continues for a short distance further before merging with the river Erdre.

Cross the canal via the bridge and head back in the direction you have just come from, but on the opposite bank. Follow the canal for 1.1km until you meet a smaller waterway joining the canal from the left. Cross over the footbridge, turn left and follow the track beside the waterway, crossing the **D69** to another footbridge after 700m. Turn left across the bridge and then turn left onto Rue de la Bunière. After 300m turn right onto Rue de la Clef des Champs, then after a further 300m take a sharp left onto a straight cycleway heading south-east.

Continue for 1km to the end of the track, then turn right and follow the road for 700m. Take the sharp left turn, then after 300m take another sharp left turn and follow this road for 300m, passing under a railway bridge, to a crossroads with the

D69. Continue straight ahead onto the quiet lane and follow it for 2.1km until Rue Monteauciel meets Route de la Gamotrie. Turn right, and then after 100m turn left onto Chemin du Melton.

After 200m, at the end of the road, turn right onto Rue du Lavoir, then after 50m take a grassy track on your right. The surface of the track soon improves, and you follow this lane for 900m until it meets a road at a T-junction. Turn left and follow the lane for 300m to another T-junction. Turn right and follow Rue du Lavoir for 700m, until it meets the D69 again.

Turn left and follow the cycle track beside the road for 300m. Turn left onto Route du Houssais and follow the well-marked route for 700m, through the village of **Les Vaux**. As you leave the village, turn left onto a cycle track and follow it through well-signed twists and turns for 2km, then turn left onto Impasse de la Hautière. Continue on the signed route for 900m until you arrive at the marina in **Sucé-sur-Erdre** (**20km, 1hr 15min**). Sucé-sur-Erdre has a pretty riverside quay, popular with river cruisers as well as cyclists, and there are several places to eat and drink along the promenade, looking out over the wide river. Head inland from the bridge along Rue de la Mairie for 100m, then turn left at the church onto Grande Rue.

After 200m, turn left onto Rue du Port and then take your first right onto Rue du Pin. At the crossroads after 200m, follow the La Vélodyssée sign straight ahead onto Rue de la Bretonnière. Don't be led astray by the cycle-route sign that points to the right towards the station.

The road soon bends to the left, then after 75m, the lane broadens slightly next to some fenced-in manhole covers. Turn right onto the easy-to-miss track. Follow the track then residential street for 400m until you meet Route du Coteaux de la Turbalière at a T-junction. Turn right and follow the road for 200m to the D69.

You now start to say goodbye to the quiet lanes, voies vertes and canal towpaths that have provided tranquil days of cycling over the first 370km of La Vélodyssée. You are entering the suburbs of the city of Nantes, and the road infrastructure reflects this. Fortunately, the cyclist is still well catered for, often with separate, dedicated cycle lanes alongside the busy road.

Turn left onto the marked cycleway that runs on the pavement on the left-hand side of the D69. The route now follows the D69 and then the D39 for 7.2km, either along a cycle lane separated from the main road by a barrier, or by taking short detours along parallel residential streets until it arrives at the interchange with the Nantes to Paris motorway, the **A11** (**28.8km, 1hr 50min**).

Follow the cycle lane under the A11, then after 1km, turn left at the roundabout onto Rue de la Haute Gournière. After 1.6km you rejoin the banks of the river Erdre. Pass under the road and railway bridges and follow the banks of the Erdre

Celebrating arrival in Nantes at a café on Place du Commerce

downstream. You briefly leave the river for a detour through the Nantes University campus, then after 5.8km, you arrive at Quay Ceineray, where the Erdre appears to terminate as it disappears beneath the soaring **Monument aux 50-Otages**.

At the roundabout, continue straight across onto the cycle lane in the middle of the road. Follow this along the tree-lined Cours des Cinquante-Otages as it sweeps round to the left following the old course of the Erdre. After 1km, having crossed five roundabouts, you arrive at the wide Boulevard Jean Philippot.

Turn right, cross over the tramlines and follow the bus and cycle lane over a roundabout. After 200m there is a double roundabout; continue straight across onto Rou Félix Eboué, signposted Ouest-Centre Ville. At the next roundabout, bear left onto Boulevard des Nations-Unies. Follow this road for 700m until you arrive at the **Passerelle Victor Schoelcher bridge** over the river Loire (**38.7km, 3hr 30min**).

NANTES

Nantes, France's sixth most populous city, is located at the confluence of three rivers: the river Loire flowing from east to west, the Erdre joining it from the north, and the Sèvre Nantaise from the south. There has been a settlement at Nantes since the Bronze Age and evidence of the Roman city can still be seen.

During the French Wars of Religion, Nantes was a Catholic stronghold. The Duke of Brittany strongly opposed the succession of the Protestant Henry IV to the throne of France and set up an independent government in Nantes. The Wars of Religion were ended by Henry IV's signing of the Edict of Nantes in 1598, which legalised Protestantism in France. Several 15th- and 16th-century half-timbered houses can be seen in the narrow streets of Nantes' medieval centre, beside the imposing Château des ducs

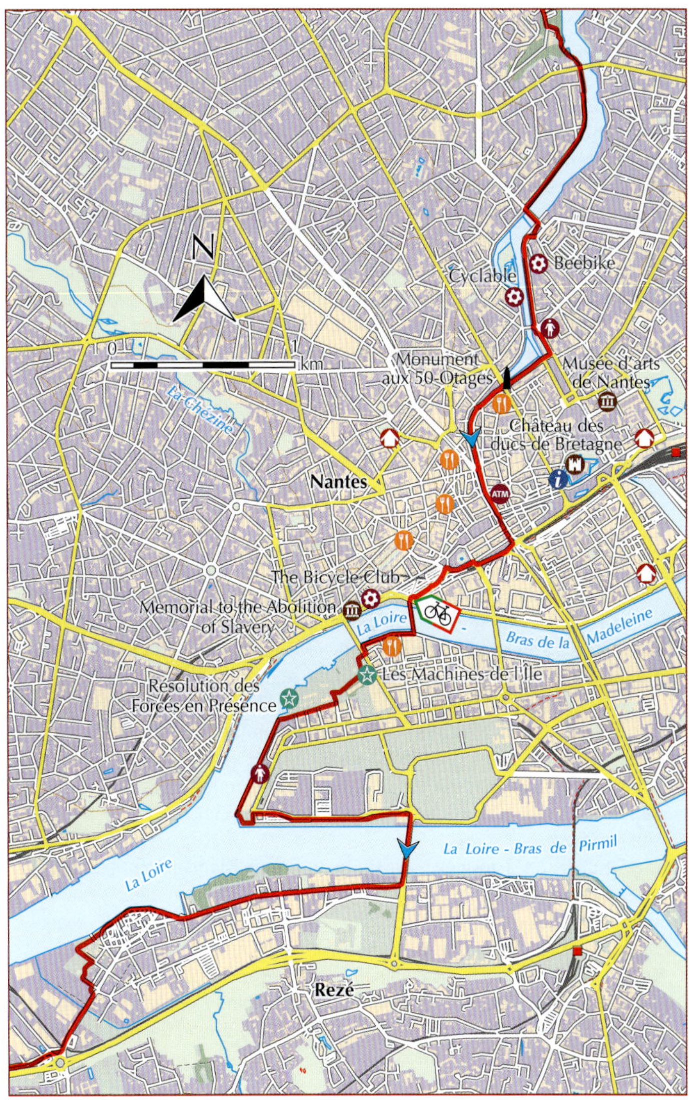
N
0
1
km
Beebike
Cyclable
Monument
aux 50-Otages
Musée d'arts
de Nantes
Château des
ducs de Bretagne
Nantes
La Chézine
ATM
The Bicycle Club
Memorial to the Abolition
of Slavery
La Loire
Bras de la Madeleine
Les Machines de l'Île
Résolution des
Forces en Présence
La Loire - Bras de Pirmil
La Loire
Rezé

de Bretagne. Work started on the Gothic cathedral in 1434 and it was completed 457 years later.

In 1706, Nantes' shipowners began trading in enslaved people, forcibly transporting 450,000 people to the Caribbean. Despite the law that was passed in 1794, freeing all French colonial enslaved people, Nantes' merchants continued operating illegally until 1827. Modern Nantes has done more than many similar European ports to recognise its involvement with this unpardonable trade. Le Mémorial de l'abolition de l'esclavage (the Memorial to the Abolition of Slavery) was opened in 2012 on the Quai de la Fosse. It starts along the quayside and then heads down steps to a large underground passage close to the water level. It is a moving and emotionally demanding experience, but if you want to understand the history of Nantes and only have time to visit one exhibition, arguably this should be it.

As Nantes expanded in the 20th century, the demand for land led to most of the river channels being filled in and their water courses altered. The river Erdre was diverted, channelled underground, and its former course turned into the thoroughfare of the Cours des 50-Otages. The Feydeau and Gloriette Islands in the old town were attached to the north bank, and the other islands in the Loire were joined together to create l'Île de Nantes.

During World War 2, the city was captured by the Germans, and in 1941 the Nazi occupiers executed 48 French civilians in retaliation for the assassination of the imposed German governor. The victims of the atrocity are commemorated in the impressive Monument aux 50-Otages. Allied bombing raids in 1943 killed 1,732 people and destroyed much of the city.

For centuries Nantes has attracted artists. JMW Turner painted *Nantes from l'Île Feydeau,* which is now on display in the Château des ducs de Bretagne. André Breton and Jacques Vaché lived in Nantes, leading to the city being described as the birthplace of surrealism. The city's Musée d'arts de Nantes also has works by Tintoretto, Brueghel, Rubens, Monet, Picasso and Kandinsky.

Situated on a former industrial site on an island in the Loire, Les Machines de l'Île is inspired by the works of Nantes-born Jules Verne, the author of *Around the World in Eighty Days* and *Twenty Thousand Leagues Under the Sea*. The park is populated with huge animated models, including the 37-tonne mechanical spider, La Princesse, an oversized fairground ride; Le Carrousel des Mondes Marins; and Le Grand Éléphant, a 12m-high elephant that can carry 52 passengers as it parades around the park spraying water at spectators.

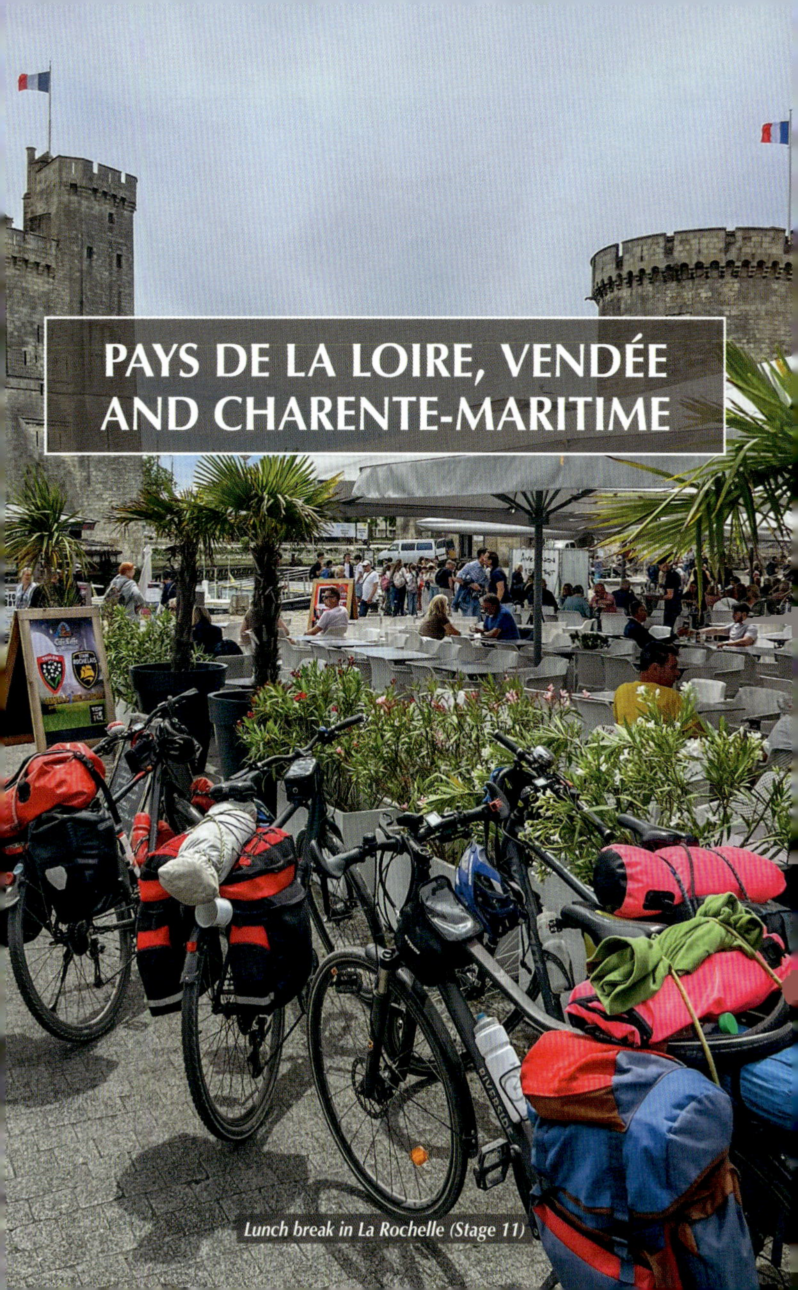

PAYS DE LA LOIRE, VENDÉE AND CHARENTE-MARITIME

Lunch break in La Rochelle (Stage 11)

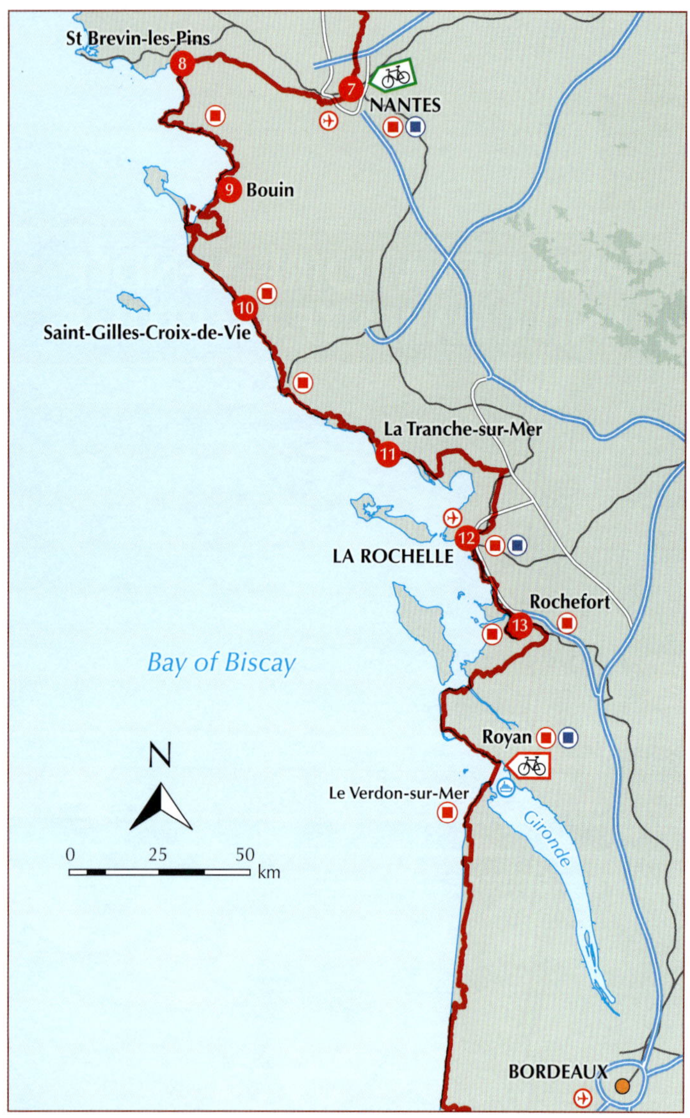
St Brevin-les-Pins
8
7
NANTES
9
Bouin
10
Saint-Gilles-Croix-de-Vie
La Tranche-sur-Mer
11
12
LA ROCHELLE
Rochefort
13
Bay of Biscay
Royan
N
Le Verdon-sur-Mer
Gironde
0
25
50
km
BORDEAUX

STAGE 7

Nantes to Saint-Brevin-les-Pins

Start	Nantes, Passerelle Victor Schoelcher bridge
Finish	Saint-Brevin-les-Pins, Place Bougainville
Time	3hr 45min
Distance	61.3km
Ascent	180m
Descent	180m
Refreshments en route	Le Pellerin, La Martinière, Le Migron and Paimboeuf
Accommodation en route	Le Migron and Paimboeuf

The route heads west along the southern bank of the Loire estuary, from Nantes to the Atlantic Ocean. There is plenty to see along the way; the post-industrial landscape has been regenerated with intriguing art installations, and the rural waterside is rich in wildlife. The stage takes you from the urban bustle of the city to the wide estuary, where the historic Royal River enters the ocean at the end of its 1000km journey across France.

Cross the river Loire using the Passerelle Victor Schoelcher cycle and pedestrian bridge, then turn right onto Quai François Mitterrand for 300m until you meet the Boulevard Léon Bureau at a flight of steps. Briefly turn left, to avoid the steps, before crossing the boulevard and entering the large open paved area of the former dockyard that now forms Les Machines de l'Île park.

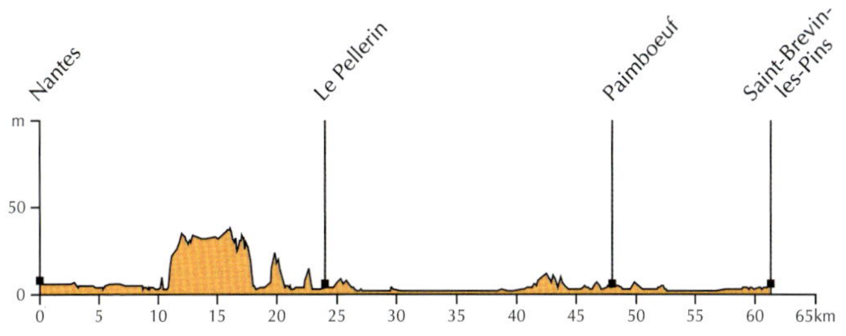

The elephant at Les Machines de l'Île, Nantes

Keep the long historic building on your left and then the Carrousel des Mondes Marins on your right until you join the Mail des Chantiers heading south-west. You pass *La Station Prouvé* and *Résolution des forces en présence*, the first two of ten Estuaire art installations that you will pass on this stage of the route.

> The **Estuaire art project** (estuaire.info/en) includes 28 large-scale public art installations on the banks of the Loire, between Nantes and Sainte-Nazaire. Estuaire contemporary art exhibitions were held along the Loire estuary in 2007, 2009 and 2012. They left behind several permanent works of art and inspired the Voyage à Nantes, a series of art exhibitions across the city, which has been held every summer since.

Follow the Mail des Chantiers until you meet the river, then turn left along the Quai des Antilles, passing Les Anneaux, until you reach the south-west tip of the island. Continue following the bank of the river, now heading briefly upstream along Quai Président Wilson, until you arrive at the **Pont des Trois-Continents bridge**. It is easy to lose the waymarked route on the Île de Nantes, but as you are on a small island in the river, if you keep following the Loire on your right, you will soon end up at the Pont des Trois-Continents.

Cross the bridge to the south bank of the Loire. At the end of the bridge, turn right onto Rue de la Basse Île and follow the road for 1.6km until the Loire comes back into view. Bear right onto Quai Robert Surcouf and follow the bank of the river for 500m until you pass *Le Pendule*. A further 800m of meandering waymarked cycle track leads to a large roundabout on the D723. The dedicated cycle lane initially runs parallel to the main road then bears right away from it. After 2.2km, you pass under the N844 as it starts its ascent to cross the Loire via the impressive Pont de Cheviré.

After 600m, the track turns left, leaving the road and following a small stream for 600m before it turns right, crosses a bridge and meets Quai de la Vallée. Turn right and follow the quiet country lane for 900m to the T-junction with Rue du Port Lavigne. Turn left, and then after 150m, turn right onto Chemin de la Rinière. After a short distance, the lane becomes a cycle track, which you follow for 600m to a tree-covered roundabout.

Turn sharp right onto Rue de la Pagerie and follow it for 1.1km until it meets Rue Beausoleil at a T-junction. Turn right, then after 300m, turn right again onto Rue de la Guérinière and follow it for 600m to a small roundabout. Turn left onto Route de la Marche and follow it for 300m to a crossroads. Go straight across to a lane that quickly becomes a cycle track through woodland. After 900m turn right and follow that track for 800m until it meets a road.

Go straight across onto Allée du 8 Mai 1945, then at the roundabout in 200m, turn right. At the next roundabout after 700m, turn left and then immediately right onto Rue de la Hibaudière. Follow the well-waymarked route through residential streets and then on a cycle track until after 2.3km, you meet Rue du Bac. Cross the road and follow the track for 200m. Turn left on Rue de la Cale, then after 400m, take the right-hand fork into a car park, bear left after the picnic table and follow the track for 1.2km until you reach Rue Jean de Martel.

Turn right, then after 300m, turn left. After 100m, turn right onto a cycle track and follow for 2.1km, past the **Château du Pé**, to the junction with Rue du Port. Turn right and follow for 300m to a roundabout, then turn right onto Rue du Bac.

After 1.3km, the Loire comes back into view at **Le Pellerin** (**24km, 1hr 30min**), where the ferry departs to the north bank of the Loire.

The route now follows the riverbank for 2.3km to **La Martinière**, where there is a steam pumping house that has been carefully restored by enthusiasts and opened to the public. Bearing right for 100m brings you to the entrance of the Canal de la Martinière, by a restaurant. It is worth taking a short detour to where the canal meets the river to see *Misconceivable*; the boat arches over the quayside as if it is irresistibly drawn towards the water.

Le Jardin Étoilé art installation at Paimboeuf

Due to the abolition of the trade in enslaved people, and the loss of trade resulting from the war with England, Nantes' importance as a port declined. The surpassing of Nantes by its upwardly mobile downstream rival, Saint-Nazaire, led to the building of the **Canal de la Martinière** to allow Nantes to remain accessible to large ships. Completed in 1892, the canal fell out of use 18 years later due to more effective dredging techniques allowing ships to use the Loire. The canal is now used for leisure and for regulating the water level of the surrounding marshland.

Follow the north bank of the maritime canal for 3.4km, first crossing the Canal de Buzay via the sluice bridge, then crossing the Canal de la Martinière, and turn immediately right. Continue along the south bank for 8.5km to **Le Migron** (**38.2km, 2hr 20min**), where there is a café and accommodation. After a further 2.6km, you reach the end of the canal at **La Cruaudais**. As the canal expands into a wide basin, just before the lock gates at its end, bear left away from the canal for 700m.

At the crossroads, turn right onto a winding country lane and follow it for 4.4km, passing the Château du Plessis-Mareil and crossing a wide unused road which was built to service a nuclear power station that was never built, until you reach a T-junction at **La Foucauderie**.

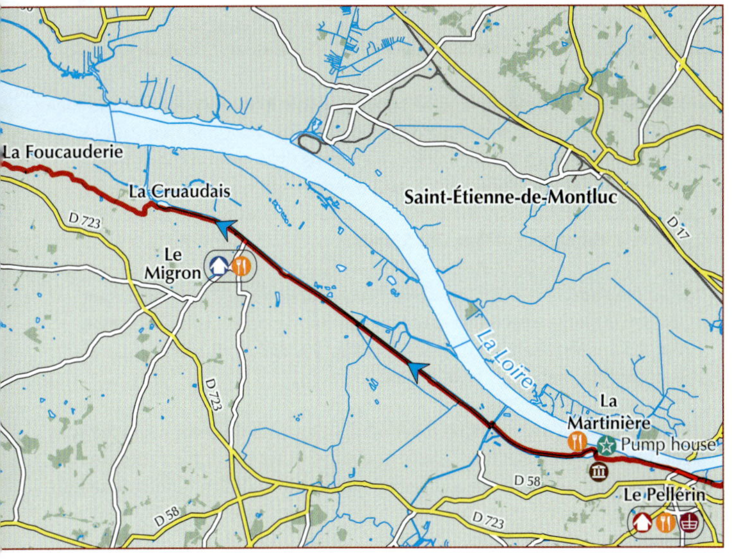

The quayside at Paimboeuf

Turn right onto Route de la Virée Longue, follow it round to the left and then after 800m, turn right at the war memorial onto Rue du Capitaine Paul Leroy. The lane soon becomes a cycle track, which turns right when it meets the D723. Continue for 900m to a roundabout with a model lighthouse in the middle. Go straight ahead for 400m until the Loire comes back into view at *Le Jardin Étoilé* art installation at **Paimboeuf** (**48km, 2hr 55min**).

From the mid-17th century onwards, **Paimboeuf** developed as an important port serving large vessels that could not pass further up the Loire. When the port at Saint-Nazaire was constructed in the 19th century, Paimboeuf started its decline into the sleepy town it is today.

Continue along the quayside, bearing right towards the river when the road is signed 'no entry', passing a bakery and cafés. After passing a campsite by a mini roundabout, you arrive at a larger roundabout after 2.2km. Continue straight ahead, taking the cycle track that runs on the left-hand side of the D77 for 1.4km to **Corsept**.

Bear left on the cycle path into the village, turn right after the walled cemetery and follow Rue de la Maison Verte until the roundabout on the D77, after 700m. Go straight ahead at the roundabout and continue for 200m to the port. Turn right onto a cycle track that follows the bank of the widening Loire for 8.3km, until you arrive below the soaring Pont de Saint-Nazaire, which carries the busy D213 over the Loire estuary. Pass under the bridge, then after 100m, turn right onto Avenue de la Brière. At the end of the road turn left onto Allée de la Loire, then after 500m, arrive at Place Bougainville in **Saint-Brevin-les-Pins** (**61.3km, 3hr 45min**).

SAINT-BREVIN-LES-PINS

The Le Débarcadère bar marks not only the end of this stage but also the start of the EV6, which heads east for 4,700km to the shore of the Black Sea in Romania.

Heading through the botanical garden to the Atlantic beach, you find the final Estuaire art installation of the route, *Le Serpent d'Océan*. The impressive snake skeleton emerges from the ocean as the tide recedes, with its sinewy form mirroring the Pont de St Nazaire as it snakes across the estuary.

The Serpent de la Océan, St-Brevin-les-Pins

STAGE 8

Saint Brevin-les-Pins to Bouin

Start	Saint Brevin-les-Pins, Place Bougainville
Finish	Bouin, Place de l'Église
Time	4hr 35min
Distance	76.8km
Ascent	330m
Descent	330m
Refreshments en route	Saint-Michel-Chef-Chef, Préfailles, Pornic and Les Moutiers-en-Retz
Accommodation en route	Préfailles, Pornic and Les Moutiers-en-Retz

This stage tours the Baie de Bourgneuf, hugging the Atlantic Ocean all the way. It is divided in two by the pretty seaside town of Pornic, perfectly placed for a lunch stop. After Pornic the route takes you through marais, low-lying marshland criss-crossed by drainage channels. This is oyster country, and the influences of this gastronomic delight are evident along the route.

Leave Place Bougainville, heading south-west for 700m, following Avenue du Bois and passing the maritime museum and a campsite. At the T-junction with Avenue Gabrielle, turn left and then first right. After 700m, brief glimpses of the sandy beach bordering the Atlantic Ocean gradually turn into an uninterrupted vista on your right-hand side, and glorious cycling on beachside cycle paths and quiet seaside roads begins.

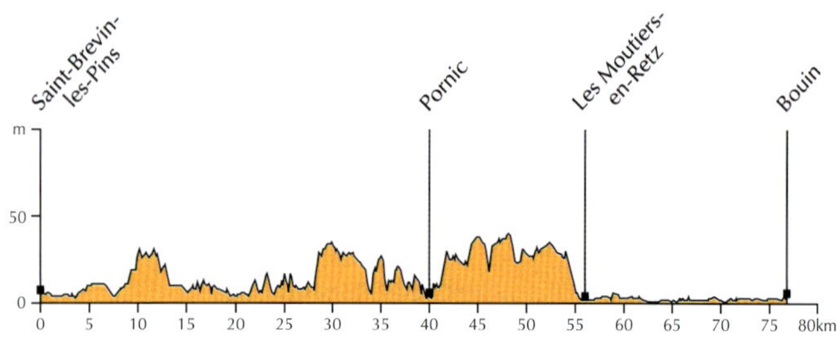

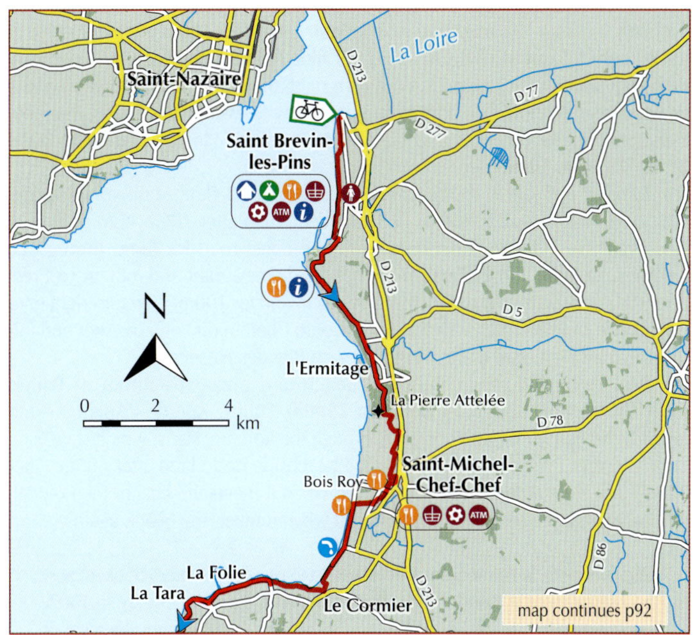

After 1km of Saint Brevin-les-Pins beach front, the road bears to the left and you take the cycle path, which continues alongside the beach for 1.2km. At the campsite, turn left and after 150m, just before the road meets the roundabout, turn right onto a cycle lane. Follow the cycle lane for 850m to the third roundabout, then turn right onto Boulevard de l'Océan. After 2.4km, at the fork in the road, bear right onto Allée des Cigales, then after 800m, bear right onto Allée Yvonne. Continue for 1.7km, initially through the holiday homes of **L'Ermitage** and then through shaded woodland along Chemin du Breneau, to the junction with Avenue de la Cathelinière. (The 2.7m-tall megalithic **Menhir de la Pierre Attelée** is now a 70m detour to your right.)

Bear right, then turn immediately left onto Rue de la Pierre Levée. After 300m, turn right onto Chemin de la Fontaine and continue onto Rue de la Roussellèrie for 600m. Just before you reach the D213, turn right onto a lane that soon becomes a track. After 500m, go straight across Route de Gohaud, take your first left and then take the second right onto a cycle track for 800m to a roundabout. Turn left onto Avenue des Renardières, then after 200m, turn right onto a cycle track before you reach the roundabout. Follow for 150m until you arrive at the church in **Saint-Michel-Chef-Chef** (**11.8km, 45min**). Turn right and continue to the T-junction with Rue du Redois. Turn right, then take your first left onto Rue du Moulin and follow for 700m to the junction with Avenue des Sports. Bear left, then at the first junction, turn right and follow Avenue de la Plage for 600m to the beach (**13.6km, 50min**).

Turn left and follow the beachside cycle lane for 2.4km. At the mini roundabout, turn right onto Avenue de la Saulzinière, then after 200m, turn right onto Boulevard de l'Océan. Continue along the coast road for 5km, through **Le Cormier**, **La Folie** and **La Tara**, to the beachside restaurant and jetty in La Prée. After the car park, follow the road as it heads inland for 100m, then turn right onto Chemin de La Prée. After 500m, turn right onto Chemin du Port aux Ânes and follow the road for 1.5km to the T-junction with Rue des Fossettes.

Turn right and reach the port, beach and pizza restaurant at **Pointe Saint-Gildas** after 800m (**24.2km, 1hr 25min**). Follow Rue de l'Apcheu south towards the lighthouse and continue through the no-entry signs, which state 'sauf vélos' (except cycles), until you join the beachside cycle lane after 600m. After 300m, turn right at the T-junction and left when it meets the beach, then repeat, turning right at the next T-junction and left when it meets the beach again.

Sémaphore de la Pointe Saint-Gildas was established as a strategic lookout post and semaphore station for maritime signalling in the Loire estuary in 1862, becoming a lighthouse in 1954. Today, a museum charts the development of maritime communications and details the shipwrecks in the Loire estuary.

View over the Port de Pêche to Château de Pornic

The next 3km follows a delightful coastal cycle track, passing several sandy coves, to the pretty beach at **Port Meleu**. Continue along the coast road for 300m, then turn left onto Rue des Anjoncs for 500m. At the crossroads, turn right onto Chemin de la Levertrie for 200m to a T-junction, then turn right and then left by the motorhome parking. Follow the winding gravel track for 900m to a crossroads. Turn right, then after 400m, turn right again and follow the road for 1.7km to the beautiful beach at **Le Portmain**.

Head inland for 100m and then turn into the beach car park and follow the track out the other side for 500m. At the T-junction, turn right, then take your first left and follow the road for 750m to the roundabout. Turn left and follow Chemin de la Madrague for 200m until it meets the D751. Turn right and follow the road for 300m to the narrow sandy inlet of **Plage du Porteau**. Follow the cycle lane along the coast road for the next 4.2km, through Sainte-Marie-sur-Mer, to the quayside in **Pornic** (**40.2km, 2hr 25min**).

PORNIC

Built at the confluence of three rivers and the sea, the town of Pornic has been inhabited since Neolithic times, and several ancient monuments can be found in the area, with the most impressive being the Tumulus des Mousseaux, a substantial excavated tomb. Coveted by the Vikings, the port and its valley were protected by a fortress. The medieval quarter, with its narrow streets, stone steps and covered market, has the Château de Pornic built at its prow, perched high on a rocky promontory.

The town expanded significantly in the 1830s due to the fashion for water sports and sea-bathing. In 1864, Robert Browning published his poem 'Gold Hair: A Legend of Pornic'. The arrival of the railway in 1875 further increased the number of summer visitors, who built elegant Belle Époque villas along the coast.

Leave Pornic on the southern side of the bay via a stunning section of coastal cycle lane, with large elegant villas to one side and views across the small boats in the bay to the castle and medieval town on the other. After 1.3km, at **Pointe de Gourmalon**, turn left onto Rue de l'Océan and follow the road for 2.3km. At the painted mini roundabout, bear left onto Rue Jules Verne for 200m, then bear right onto Rue des Jardins. Continue for 200m, through the no-entry sign, which states 'sauf riverains et cycles' (except residents and cycles), to a cycle track.

Follow the track for 500m until immediately before it meets Rue de la Font aux Bretons, where a cycle track leads off to the right. Follow this for 300m to a mini roundabout. Go straight ahead and follow Rue du Meunier le Clion for 500m, then turn right onto Rue René-Guy Cadou and follow it for 1.5km to the white memorial cross at the **Croix de Nourettes** crossroads.

Go straight across, then after 100m, turn right immediately after the public toilet. Follow the lane, which soon becomes cycles only, for 800m. Turn left onto Avenue du Petit Bois Moisan, go over the railway bridge, turn left onto Avenue des Paons, then turn right onto Avenue de la Noue Fleurie. After 300m, turn right onto the cycle lane and follow it for 500m to Avenue Gilbert Burlot. Turn left and continue for 700m to the sail-less windmill, Le Moulin Dousset. Turn left onto Rue René-Guy Cadou. After 50m turn right by the crucifix onto Rue de la Jaginière (**50km, 3hr**).

After 1km, turn left and pass underneath the D13 to a T-junction after 400m. Turn left, then after 400m, almost double back on yourself onto a cycle track and follow this for 2.2km to a crossroads. Turn right and follow the lane for 1.7km, over the D13 and into the pretty village of **Les Moutiers-en-Retz** (**55.5km, 3hr 20min**), with cafés offering shaded outside tables overlooking the village square and the church.

Head south past the church, bear right then left, and go over the level crossing. After 200m, before arriving at the beach, the road bears left

A carrelet *stranded by the tide at Les Moutiers-en-Retz*

onto Route du Collet. Follow this road for 1.5km through the marais to a road junction. Bear right and continue for 3km to **Port du Collet** (**60.2km, 3hr 35min**).

For centuries, the picturesque harbour at **Port du Collet** was a major port exporting salt produced from the local coastal marshes. It is now a centre for the oyster-farming industry, and there are several restaurants serving local huîtres (oysters) fresh from the ocean.

For those who can carry or push their bikes up the steps, it is possible to use the passerelle (footbridge) to cross the river. For everyone else, the waymarked route heads inland along the bank of the Falleron then bears left to follow the Étier de la Charreau Blanche for 600m. It then crosses the water, heads back for 600m on the other bank, then crosses the Falleron. This is the border between the departments of the Loire-Atlantique and Vendée, and you may notice that the local branding on the waymarking signs changes as you cross the river from one department to the other.

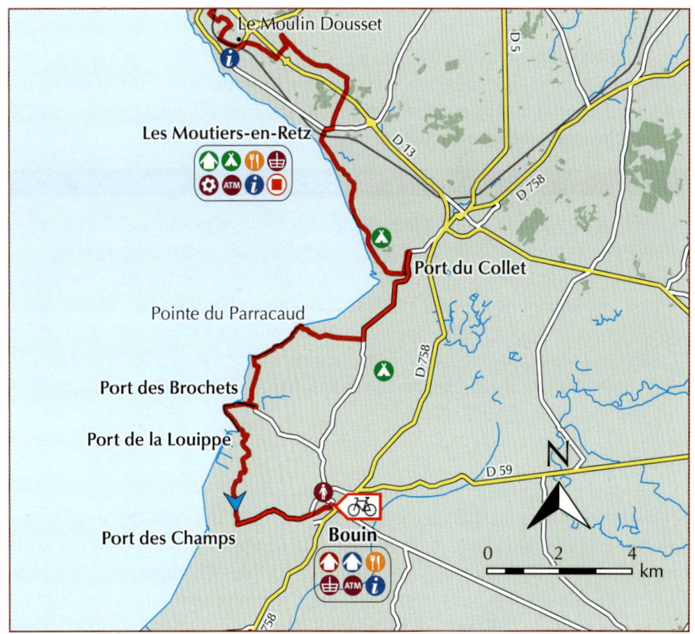

Low-lying fields lined with poppies under a big sky, Bouin

Follow the Polder de Saint-Céran for 2km, then turn right onto a gravel track and follow it for 2.2km to the sea at **Pointe du Parracaud**. Turn left and follow the track for 1.6km to a car park. Turn left and follow the track for another 1.6km to **Port des Brochets** (**69km, 4hr 10min**).

CARRELETS

Arriving in the port along the Étier des Brochets, you will see dozens of little sheds on stilts, with large square nets on pulleys hanging in front of them. These are carrelets, named after the filet carré (square net), the primary implement of the hut. They were developed in the 18th century by fishermen, to avoid getting wet. The now-familiar silhouette of carrelets, with their walkways back to dry land, appeared in the early 1900s, and they are ubiquitous on this section of the route. They are a popular leisure activity and some can be hired.

Cross the bridge over the Étier des Brochets and head west towards the sea. Follow the coastline for 2km to a T-junction. Turn right and cross the small bridge with the old wooden sluice gate at **Port de la Louippe**. Turn left onto the cycle track and follow for 2.8km to a crossroads in **Port des Champs**. Leave the waymarked route by turning left before crossing the bridge and follow the lane for 2.8km to the centre of **Bouin** (**76.8km, 4hr 35min**).

STAGE 9

Bouin to Saint-Gilles-Croix-de-Vie

Start	Bouin, Place de l'Église
Finish	Saint-Gilles-Croix-de-Vie railway station
Time	4hr 30min
Distance	72.6km
Ascent	130m
Descent	130m
Variant route	L'Île de Noirmoutier via the Passage du Gois, reducing stage length by 10.5km (14km, +10m/-10m, 50min)
Refreshments en route	Beauvoir-sur-Mer, Fromentine and Saint-Jean-de-Monts
Accommodation en route	Beauvoir-sur-Mer, Fromentine and Saint-Jean-de-Monts

The route starts by weaving its way through marais to the sea at Fromentine. It then meanders along cycle tracks, through sand dunes, pine forests, and seaside towns, before arriving at the port of Saint-Gilles-Croix-de-Vie. A variant to the route takes you across the historic Passage du Gois to the sandy island of L'Île de Noirmoutier before rejoining the waymarked route on the mainland, via a lofty bridge.

From the centre of Bouin, retrace the final 2.8km of Stage 8 by following Route du Port des Champs to the crossroads. Turn left, cross over the bridge, then turn immediately right and continue west along the south bank of the Étier des Champs,

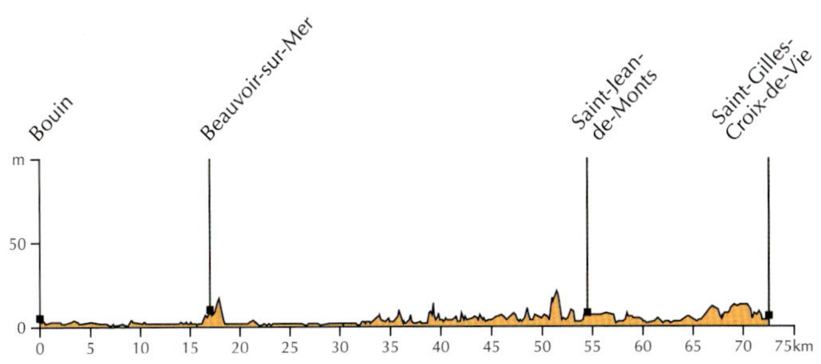

towards the sea. Follow the track for 3km along the Polder du Daim, then turn left and head inland for 300m. Turn right and follow the track for 2.8km to **Port du Bec**.

Cross the bridge with the sluice gate over Le Dain and follow the D51 for 1km. Turn right onto Les Alais and follow the lane for 1.2km to rejoin the D51 at La Croix Rouge. Turn right then left onto the D948, and then right onto **La Croix Rouge**, just before the car park with shaded picnic benches. Follow the road for 800m to a T-junction, turn right and follow the lane for 300m to a turning on the left (**12.4km, 45min**).

> You now have a choice: the waymarked route turns left and heads inland via Beauvoir-sur-Mer before rejoining the coast at Fromentine. Alternatively, continuing ahead on the **variant route** leads to L'Île de Noirmoutier via the legendary 4.2km Passage du Gois. It then follows the island's coast before returning to the mainland over the Pont de Noirmoutier to rejoin the waymarked route after 14km. The variant reduces the stage length by 10.5km, but the causeway can only be crossed 1½hr either side of low tide.

To continue on the waymarked route, turn left and follow the road for 1.7km to the D948. Cross over the road and continue on Marais Buor for 600m to a gravel crossroads. Turn right and follow the track between the marais for 1.2km to a T-junction. Turn right onto Rue de la Coquille and follow it for 700m to the centre of **Beauvoir-sur-Mer** (**16.6km, 1hr**).

Turn right, between the tourist information office and the town hall, onto Rue des Écoles. After 200m, turn left onto Rue du Puits Pineau. In a further 200m, continue straight across at the crossroads by the cemetery onto Avenue des Moulins. Follow for 800m to the old windmill, then turn right onto Chemin du Saint-Esprit and follow for 500m until you reach the marais.

Bear left then right onto La Petite Maladrie and follow for 4km to **Saint-Urbain**. Turn right at the mini roundabout, then after 300m, turn right onto Rue de la Sablière. Follow for 1.3km, then turn left opposite the crucifix onto Les Cochets. Follow this meandering road, crossing straight across the D51, for 6.3km to the Ecomuseum Le Daviaud. Continue for a further 900m to a T-junction. Cross the road to the cycle track and follow for 1.3km to the roundabout in **La Barre-de-Monts** (**32.5km, 2hr**).

At the roundabout bear right onto Avenue de l'Estacade, then turn immediately right onto a narrow track. Bear left on Chemin de la Joséphine and follow for 300m until it rejoins the D22. Turn right, then after 400m, turn left onto Route de La Darotte for 400m. Turn right onto Rue des Chênes Verts, which soon becomes a cycle track. Follow this for 1.5km to the harbour at **Fromentine** (**35.5km, 2hr 10min**).

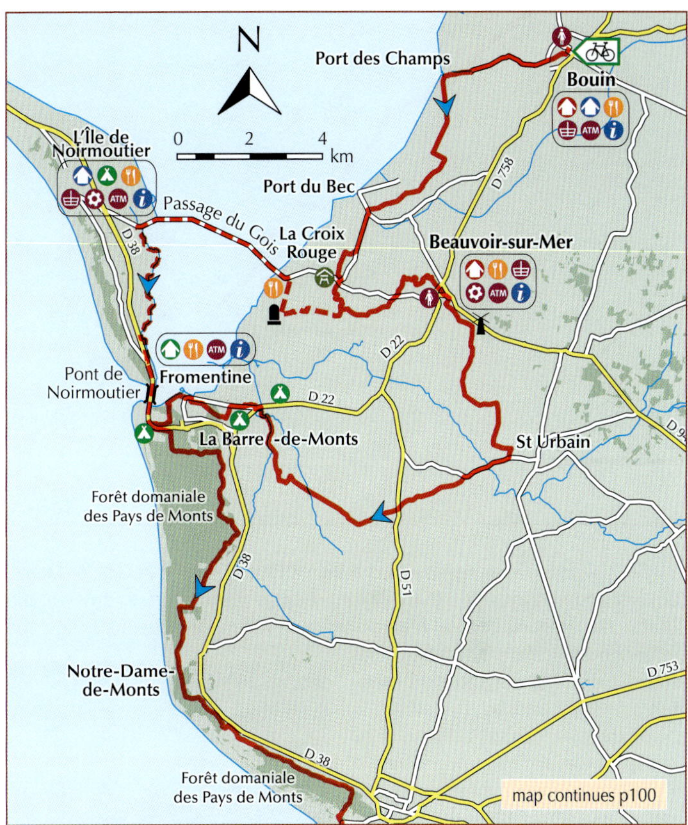

Turn left and cycle along the esplanade for 400m towards the impressive Pont de Noirmoutier. Turn left before the sailing school, then turn right onto a cycle track. Follow the track for 1.1km until it passes under the road bridge. Turn left and follow the track to where it joins the variant route cycle track (**36.9km, 2hr 15min**).

Continue for 2.4km to a track junction. Turn right before the track meets the road and head south. The well-waymarked track meanders through pine forests and campsites until you arrive at Avenue de la Mer in **Notre-Dame-de-Monts** after 6.6km (**46km, 2hr 40min**).

Go straight ahead and follow the track for 7.6km to Avenue des Pay de Monts. Turn left and continue for 700m, passing a large roundabout, to arrive at the beachside esplanade of **Saint-Jean-de-Monts** (**54.6km, 3hr 20min**). Follow the esplanade for 2.8km, with a beautiful sandy beach to your right and beach-front hotels and cafés to your left.

At the roundabout at the end of the esplanade, the track heads inland for 200m to a bigger roundabout and then bears right. Follow the track as it once more weaves between sand dunes, pine forests and campsites for 9.5km until it meets Avenue de la Forêt in **Saint-Hilaire-de-Riez**.

Turn right and follow the cycle lane for 1.3km to the sea. Continue along the seafront for 4.5km, passing the Grosse Terre lighthouse, to arrive at the railway station in **Saint-Gilles-Croix-de-Vie** (**72.6km, 4hr 30min**).

Coming to the end of the Passage du Gois, L'Île de Noirmoutier (variant)

Feu de Grosse Terre lighthouse, Saint-Gilles-Croix-de-Vie

Variant: L'Île de Noirmoutier via the Passage du Gois

Continue along Route de la Gesière for 150m, then turn right. Follow the lane for 1km until just after a left bend. Turn right onto Le Grand Ped and follow for 750m to the T-junction by the Crosnière-Notre-Dame-Du-Pé. Turn right, then after 1km, turn left onto the D948 and follow for 400m to the Passage du Gois.

Cross the causeway, then after 200m, turn left onto a cycle track that hugs the coastline and continue for 4.4km to a roundabout on the D38. Follow the protected cycle lane that runs parallel to the D38, over the dramatic Pont de Noirmoutier, for 2km until the cycle track rejoins the waymarked route (**14km, 50min**).

PASSAGE DU GOIS

Cycling the 4.2km-long Passage du Gois, as the tide recedes to reveal the causeway in front of you, is a unique experience. The surface is paved but uneven and slippery in places. The causeway connects L'Île de Noirmoutier with the mainland and can be crossed 1hr 30min before or after low tide. Tide times are posted on a board but check online (maree.info/120) to avoid delays.

The causeway has been in use since the 18th century, with its popularity fluctuating depending on the available alternative options to reach the island, such as the ferry from Fromentine or the modern Pont de Noirmoutier. It was used in Stage 2 of the 1999 Tour de France, creating controversy when a crash on the causeway caused a 6min split in the peloton, which had a significant impact on the outcome of the race. It was used again on the Tour in 2011.

STAGE 10

Saint-Gilles-Croix-de-Vie to La Tranche-sur-Mer

Start	Saint-Gilles-Croix-de-Vie railway station
Finish	Tranche-sur-Mer, supermarket roundabout
Time	5hr 10min
Distance	81.5km
Ascent	240m
Descent	240m
Refreshments en route	Bretignolles-sur-Mer, Les Sables-d'Olonne and Jard-sur-Mer
Accommodation en route	Les Sables-d'Olonne and Jard-sur-Mer

The route meanders through forest and alongside sandy beaches to the world sailing capital and smart seaside resort of Les Sables-d'Olonne, ideally placed for a lunch stop. More shady forests and sandy tracks, with the ocean never far away to your right, lead to the seaside holiday town of La Tranche-sur-Mer.

From the railway station, continue along the quayside for 700m to the bridge over the river Vie. Cross the bridge, turn right onto the quayside and follow for 600m to a roundabout by a bridge. Go straight ahead and follow the cycle lane, with the river Jaunay on your right, for 3.2km to another bridge. Cross the bridge and turn left onto Rue du Pont du Jaunay. Follow the cycle track, which meanders through

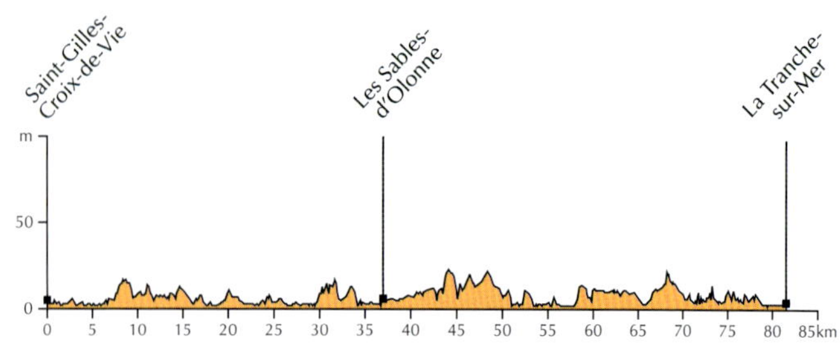

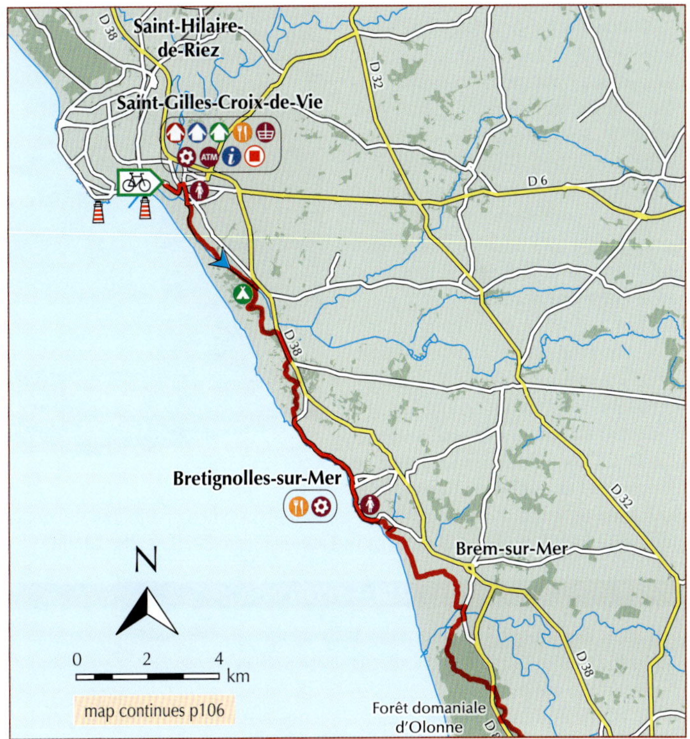

the sand dunes for 5km until it meets the sea. The cycle lane now runs next to the beach for 6.2km, through **Bretignolles-sur-Mer**, to a car park (**15.7km, 1hr**).

Turn left, heading inland towards **Brem-sur-Mer**, and continue for 800m to a roundabout. Turn right onto Rue du Calvaire, then after 600m, bear right onto Rue de l'Auzance for 600m. At the T-junction, turn left onto Rue des Gabelous for 200m to a T-junction with Route des Sables. Turn right, cross over the river, continue for 200m, then turn right onto Rue des Granges. After 900m, the road curves to the right and the route continues straight ahead onto a cycle track. Follow the track for 2km until it passes under the D80 via an underpass. Turn right and follow the lane and cycle track alongside the marais for 3.1km until it meets the D80. Cross over the pedestrian crossing and continue straight ahead onto the cycle track.

Follow the twisting track for 2km to Sauveterre and turn left onto the cycle track directly before the holiday complex. Follow the track for 3.2km as it weaves its way through the waterways of the marais to a T-junction with Rue de la Forgerie. Turn right, cross over the bridge and continue to the T-junction. Cross straight over the road onto a track and follow for 2.5km until it meets the sea at **Plage de l'Aubraie**.

A popular meeting point, Les Sables-d'Olonne

Turn left and follow the track, initially along the beach, and then inland, for 2.1km to a roundabout. Go straight across the roundabout and follow the Boulevard du Souvenir Français, alongside Port Olona, to Boulevard de l'Île Vertime in **Les Sables-d'Olonne**. Turn right, then right again next to the tourist information office and follow the quayside for 2.9km to its end at the start of La Grande Plage (**37.1km, 2hr 20min**).

LES SABLES-D'OLONNE

Built by Benedictine monks in the 11th century, the Prieuré Saint-Nicolas and the Abbaye Saint-Jean d'Orbestier have both been recently restored and are open to the public.

By the 15th century, Les Sables-d'Olonne was a major fishing port, and the Tour d'Arundel lighthouse was constructed to mark the entrance to the harbour. In the 16th century, the fishing industry centred on whaling and cod, but by the 19th century, tuna and sardines were the main focus, with canneries spreading along both sides of the channel to process the catch.

The town's fortunes flourished again in 1866 with the arrival of the railway, and the fashion for sea-bathing attracted the aristocracy and artistic elite to the Grand Plage. The Remblai, which was originally built to protect the town from the ravages of the sea, soon became a popular promenade. An eclectic collection of large seaside villas spread along the seafront, and Gustave Eiffel designed the Grand Casino de la Plage. The Remblai was modernised in the 1950s with the creation of three semi-circular rotundas and the iconic four-sided clock tower.

The beach at Les Sables-d'Olonne

To sailing enthusiasts around the world, Les Sables-d'Olonne signifies one thing: the Vendée Globe yacht race. The single-handed, round-the-world sailing race takes place every four years. It was first held in 1989, when 13 yachts left Les Sables-d'Olonne and only 7 had completed the race three months later. In 2025 a new race record was set: fewer than 65 days to sail the 45,000km around the globe. The 18m yachts cost around €8 million to build and can be seen in the Vendée Globe Village during the build-up to the event.

In 2024, a semi-submerged sculpture representing Odysseus tied to the mast of his ship, to resist the lure of the Sirens, was inaugurated. The statue faces the exit of the Port Olona Channel and is revealed or concealed as the tide ebbs and flows. Spotting scopes to view the statue can be found on the Promenade Georges Clemenceau, along which La Vélodyssée travels.

The Grande Plage is indeed a big beach, and the excellent cycle lane follows the seafront for the next 6.4km. At a small roundabout near **Abbaye Saint-Jean-d'Orbestier** the cycle track bears right and then heads inland for 1.3km before returning to the sea after 1.7km at the Baie de Cayola. Follow Rue de Cayola for 700m to where the road forks. Follow the cycle lane as it heads inland for 1.2km, passing a tree-covered roundabout, to a second roundabout. Go straight across and follow Avenue de la Mine for 2.4km to the shops, cafés and a bakery next to the route at **Port Bourgenay** (**49.5km, 3hr 5min**).

Continue along Avenue de la Plage for 800m, then turn left and follow Le Veillon for 1km to a bridge. Cross the bridge, then bear right onto a gravel track.

The track weaves through sections of marais and farmland for 2.1km to a crossroads among open fields. Turn right onto Rue de la Bourie, then continue for 700m to a crossroads with the D108 in **La Guittière**.

Go straight across onto Rue du Bitord, passing the no-entry sauf cycles sign, following the road to the left to a fork in the road after 200m. Bear right onto Rue des Courpes and follow for 2.6km. After the lane crosses the bridge over the river Payré, and then curves to the left, turn right. Follow the lane, which soon becomes a cycle track, for 1.7km through the marais until just after the lane joins Route de la Caserne des Saulnier. Turn right, then after 1.5km, turn left onto Route de l'Abbaye du Lieu Dieu and follow for 2.7km to **Jard-sur-Mer** (**62.8km, 3hr 55min**).

Leave the town on Rue du Fief l'Abbesse and follow for 2.2km to **Saint-Vincent-sur-Jard**. Turn right, then after 300m, at a small, cobbled roundabout, bear left onto the cycle lane towards Maison de Clemenceau. Follow the cycle track for 5.2km to a T-junction with Chemin de Grandes Plantes.

The promenade at Les Sables-d'Olonne

Turn left and follow the cycle lane for 600m. When the cycle lane crosses over the road, turn right onto a cycle track, which meanders pleasantly through the trees for 3.2km to the beach at **Plage des Conches**. Turn left, then after 100m, turn right onto Chemin de la Forêt and follow for 1.9km to a roundabout with a lone tree in the middle. Continue straight across, then after 100m, turn right and then immediately bear left. At the crossroads in 100m, turn left. Take the cycle track for 5.5km, sometimes snaking through the forest, and at others following a cycle path parallel to the D105, to a large roundabout and a supermarket in **La Tranche-sur-Mer** (**81.5km, 5hr 10min**).

STAGE 11

La Tranche-sur-Mer to La Rochelle

Start	La Tranche-sur-Mer, supermarket roundabout
Finish	La Rochelle railway station
Time	3hr 45min
Distance	71.5km
Ascent	80m
Descent	80m
Refreshments en route	L'Aiguillon-sur-Mer, Saint-Michel-en-l'Herm and Marans
Accommodation en route	L'Aiguillon-sur-Mer, Saint-Michel-en-l'Herm and Marans

This stage of river and canal-side paths among the marais passes through the inland port town of Marans, which makes an ideal lunch stop, with its shops and street cafés beside the river, before following the canal to the sea at the historic port of La Rochelle. There is lots to see and do at La Rochelle so this may be a day to finish the stage in good time.

From the roundabout next to the supermarket in La Tranche-sur-Mer, head north-east on a cycle lane next to the road for 500m to a second roundabout. Turn right and follow the cycle lane alongside the D46 for 4.4km to a third roundabout. Turn right, then after 300m, turn left at a roundabout by a campsite and follow the Route de La Tranche-sur-Mer for 4.1km to La Faute-sur-Mer.

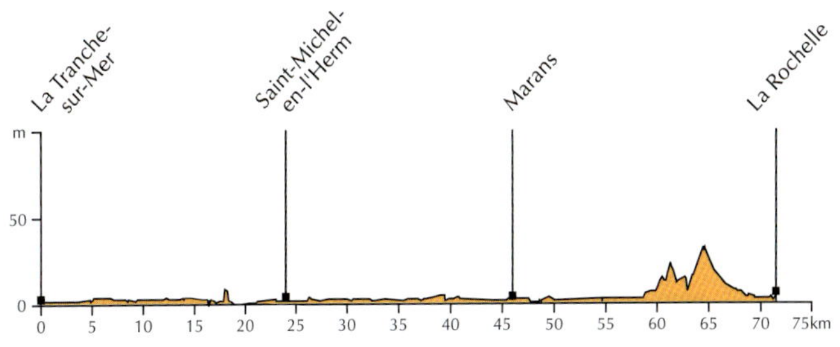

Crossing the river Lay at L'Aiguillon-la-Presqu'île

Turn left at the roundabout and cross the river Lay via the separate bridge into **L'Aiguillon-sur-Mer** (**9.4km, 30min**). Turn immediately right onto the quayside, with the fresh seafood and fishing equipment shops, arriving at the swimming lake after 900m. Take the path on the right, between the lake and the river, and follow it around the lake for 600m until you meet Avenue Amiral Courbet. Turn right and follow the river Lay for 5.4km to the river estuary. Turn left, heading inland for 900m to the unusual rocky outcrop settlement of **Rocher de la Dive** (**17.1km, 55min**).

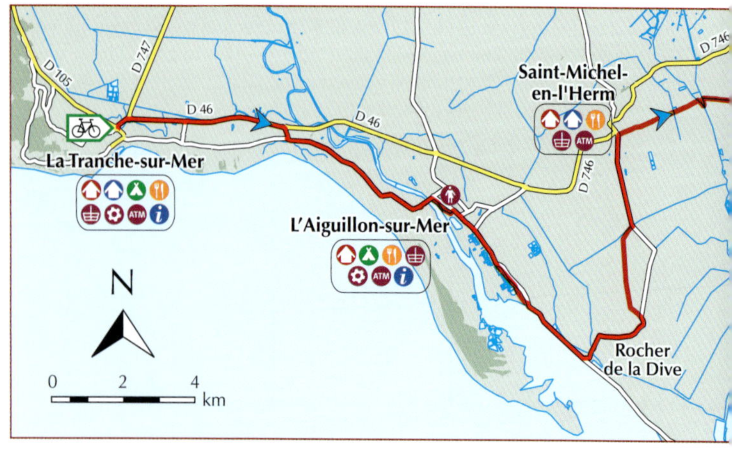

The **Rocher de la Dive** outcrop was formed 150 million years ago, when sediments were deposited in a depression in the Jurassic marls; this soft stone was eroded by rivers, creating the island, which remained until the surrounding area was drained for farmland at the beginning of the 19th century. La Dive was used as an outlook by monks from the Abbey at Saint-Michel-en-l'Herm, and a hermit's cave was dug to accommodate the sentry monk. The entrances to the cave can be found on the north side of the outcrop.

Continue for 4.2km to a T-junction, turn left and follow the lane and cycle track for 2.5km to **Saint-Michel-en-l'Herm** (**23.8km, 1hr 15min**). Turn right at a narrow pool onto Chemin du Pont Bonnit. Follow the quiet lane and cycle track, through a landscape of low-lying farmland and water-filled drainage channels, for 12.4km to the small sluice bridge at **Port de l'épine**. Continue for 1.1km to a fork in the lane, bear right and follow the lane for 2.2km to the cantilever bridge at **Pont du Brault** (**39.5km, 2hr 5min**).

Take the underpass below the D10, follow the cycle track round to the left, then turn sharp right after 500m. Follow the track for 600m to the old bridge over the Sèvre Niortaise. Cross the bridge, leaving behind the department of Vendée, and enter Charente-Maritime. Cross a second bridge over the Canal maritime de Marans à la mer, then turn left onto the canal-side path. Follow the arrow-straight path for 5.2km to the junction of the two canals on the outskirts of the riverside town of **Marans** (**46.2km, 2hr 30min**).

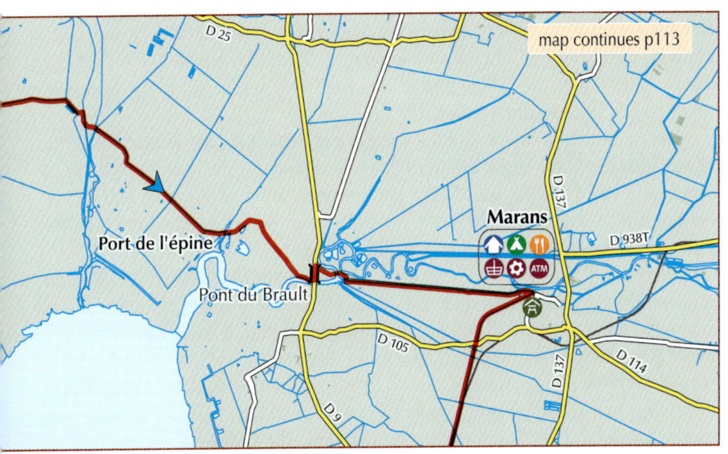

The Quai des Fusiliers, Marans (photo: Penelope Jackson)

Turn sharp right at the picnic tables by the sailing club onto the towpath of the Canal de Marans à La Rochelle. Follow the towpath for 2.5km to the aqueduct over the Canal Blanche. Continue for 4.5km to Écluses d'Andilly, at the junction with the Canal du Curé. Continue along the canal for 1.6km to the Pont des Prieurs, pass under the bridge and follow the canal for 4.7km to the bridge at **Mouillepied** (**59.5km, 3hr 10min**).

Staying on the same bank of the canal, bear right along the lane towards the village and after 50m, turn left onto Chemin des Epinettes. The lane soon becomes a track and you follow this for 500m until it meets the road. Turn left and follow the lane for 600m. Bear right at the junction, then continue along the lane for 800m to **Dompierre-sur-Mer** (**61.4km, 3hr 15min**).

Cross the bridge over the busy N11, turn left onto Rue des Hérissons, then turn immediately left again onto a narrow gravel track before the first house. Follow the track for 500m to Avenue de la Libération, turn left and then turn right, before the road crosses over the canal, onto the Canal de Marans à La Rochelle towpath. Follow the canal for 9.1km to the centre of **La Rochelle**. At Boulevard Joffre, turn left, cross the bridge over the wide canal basin and continue to the impressively grand 1920s railway station (**71.5km, 3hr 45min**).

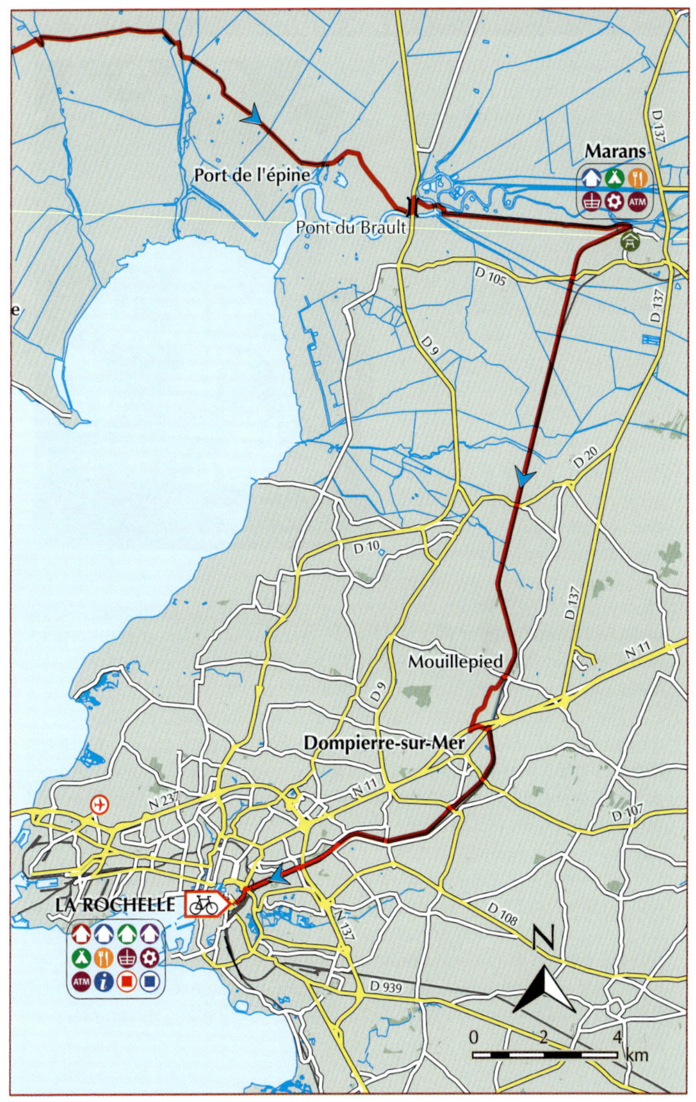
Marans
D 137
Port de l'épine
Pont du Brault
D 105
D 137
D 9
D 20
D 10
D 137
Mouillepied
N 11
D 9
Dompierre-sur-Mer
N 237
N 11
D 107
LA ROCHELLE
N 137
D 108
N
D 939
0
2
4
km

LA ROCHELLE

Cafés lining the quayside in the old port, La Rochelle

La Rochelle is a town with a long and tumultuous history. As you walk around the picturesque old port, with its abundance of restaurants, bars and cafés, the view is dominated by the three medieval towers guarding the entrance to the harbour: the Chain, Lantern and Saint Nicolas towers.

La Rochelle was granted a charter as a free port in 1130, and the Knights Templar established the Cour de la Commanderie in the centre of the city when they were awarded tax exemptions and given property by Eleanor of Aquitaine. When Eleanor married Henry Plantagenet (later Henry II) in 1152, La Rochelle came under English control, and Henry ordered the building of Vauclair Castle, remains of which are still visible in the Place de Verdun. For the next 300 years, La Rochelle was the largest French harbour on the Atlantic coast, trading in wine, salt and cheese.

The city was a Huguenots stronghold during the Wars of Religion and repeatedly came into conflict with the Catholic French crown. In 1627, Louis XIII declared the suppression of the Huguenot rebellion as his biggest priority, resulting in the 14-month siege of La Rochelle, a story that will be familiar to fans of *The Three Musketeers*. The Revocation of the Edict of Nantes in 1685 resulted in many Huguenots emigrating to America.

For over two centuries, the merchants from La Rochelle were second only to those in Nantes for their volume of trade in enslaved people, forcibly transporting 130,000 Africans to the Caribbean. The Musée du Nouveau Monde, housed in a mansion built from the proceeds of the trade, chronicles La Rochelle's involvement. The thought-provoking statue 'Clarisse, Nourrice Esclave' can be found on Allée Aimé Césaire, overlooking the entrance to the harbour.

In 1864, La Rochelle saw the maiden voyage of the *Plongeur*, the world's first mechanically powered submarine. Seventy-five years later, during World War 2, the Germans established a submarine base in La Rochelle. When French troops entered the city in 1945, after an eight-month siege, it became the final French city to be liberated. The submarine base has featured in the movies *Das Boot* and *Raiders of the Lost Ark*.

Many school pupils will have first encountered La Rochelle in their *Tricolore* French textbooks, as it is the home of the fictional Martine Dhome.

STAGE 12

La Rochelle to Rochefort

Start	La Rochelle railway station
Finish	Rochefort, Écluse du Bassin du Commerce
Time	2hr 35min
Distance	50km
Ascent	120m
Descent	120m
Refreshments en route	Châtelaillon-Plage and Saint-Laurent-de-la-Prée
Accommodation en route	Châtelaillon-Plage and Saint-Laurent-de-la-Prée

This stage explores the sandy beaches and seaside holiday towns between the two historic ports of La Rochelle and Rochefort. The route passes the intriguing historic transporter bridge, well worth a pause.

From La Rochelle railway station, cross Boulevard Joffre and head down Avenue du Général de Gaulle for 100m, then turn left onto Avenue de Colmar. After 250m, you arrive at the old dock. Turn right onto Quai de la Georgette and continue to the tourist information office. This marks the start of La Vélo Francette, a cycle route that runs for 600km between La Rochelle and the Normandy port of Ouistreham.

Turn left onto Quai Georges Simenon, cycle along the quay, between the street cafés and the luxury yachts, then at the end of the harbour, turn left and cross the bridge over the dock entrance. Turn right after the bridge onto Avenue Michel Crépeau and follow for 1.4km to a roundabout. Turn right onto Avenue des Minimes

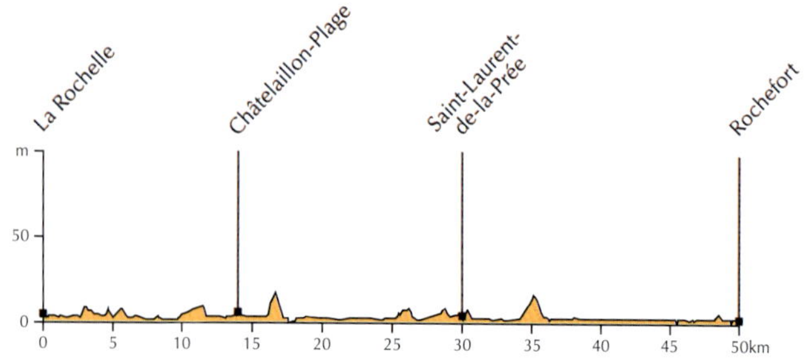

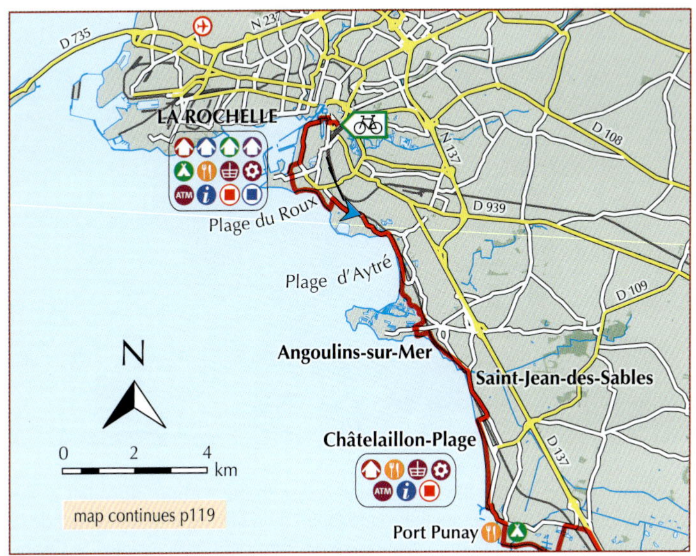

and follow it along the quayside. After 500m, when the quayside cycle lane turns right to follow the water, you turn left onto Rue de la Sauvagère (this turning is very easy to miss) and follow the road for 550m until it reaches the sea.

Turn left and follow a cycle track alongside **Plage du Roux** for 1.2km to the end of the beach. Follow the cycle track as it heads inland for 200m to a T-junction, turn right and follow the cycle lane for 1.9km until it meets the railway track at Plage d'Aytré station. Turn right onto a cycle track just before the level crossing and follow for 1km to a car park. Turn right and follow the cycle track for 600m to the end of **Plage d'Aytré**.

Turn left and follow the cycle track inland for 1km to **Angoulins-sur-Mer** train station. Continue on the cycle track for 500m to a roundabout. Turn left then immediately right onto Rue des Pois Bons and follow for 200m to the sea. Turn left onto Rue du Chay and follow for 300m to the railway track. Turn right and follow the cycle track that runs parallel to the railway for 1.4km to the beach car park at **Saint-Jean-des-Sables** (**11.8km, 35min**).

Take the tunnel under the railway, turn right before reaching the roundabout and follow the cycle track for 1.5km to a roundabout. Follow the track right onto Rue Georges Charbonneau, passing over the level crossing and arriving at **Châtelaillon-Plage** (**13.7km, 40min**) after 300m.

The casino at the beach in Châtelaillon-Plage

Turn left and follow the seafront for 2.3km to the harbour. Turn left at the sailing club, go straight across the roundabout, then turn right onto Avenue de la Falaise and follow for 600m to a roundabout. Turn right onto Avenue de l'Abbé Guichard to arrive at the beach at **Port Punay** after 600m. Turn left and follow the promenade, with its brightly painted seafront buildings, for 1.6km. Turn left after the Cuban bar with a pool, before the carrelets, and follow Chemin de l'Oasis for 800m to a T-junction.

Turn right and follow the road as it runs alongside the D137 dual carriageway until, after 2.5km, you pass underneath it. Continue for 600m, then, after crossing a bridge over a drainage channel, turn right. Follow the road as it runs parallel to the railway until it passes over a level crossing after 2.6km. Continue on the road for 700m, around a short one-way-system, before arriving at the D137 road interchange at Yves.

Turn left before the first slip road and follow the lane adjacent to the east-side of the D137 for 3.6km to the railway station at **Saint-Laurent-de-la-Prée** (**29.7km, 1hr 30min**). Turn right at the roundabout before the station and follow the cycle lane for 700m. After passing under the D137, turn left. The quiet lane runs adjacent to the not-so-quiet D137 for 4.5km to a crossroads. Turn right onto the D214 and follow the road for 1.5km, through the village of **Vergeroux**. Just before the large roundabout, turn right onto a cycle track and follow for 1.5km until just before another roundabout. Turn right again onto Rue des Pêcheurs d'Islande and follow for 700m to the banks of the **river Charente** (**38.6km, 2hr**).

Quiet lane between fields near Yves

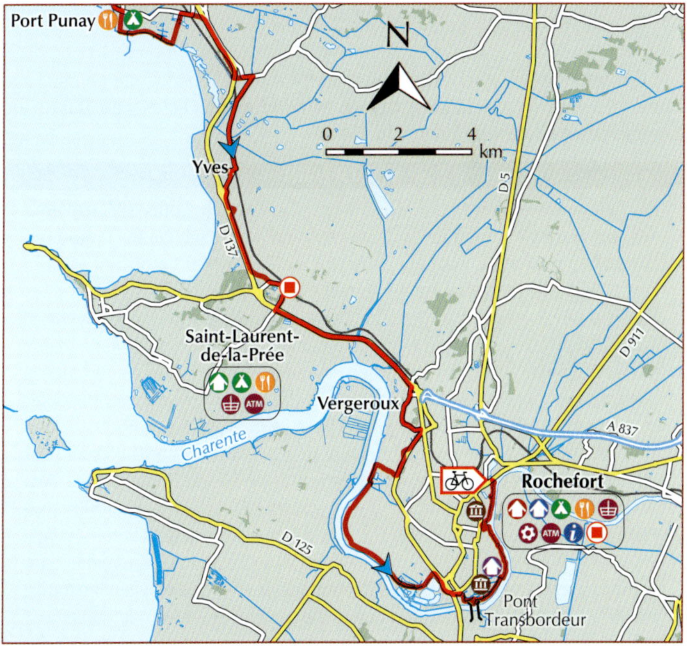

Turn left onto the riverside cycle track. Once you've rounded the bend in the river, the view is dominated by two bridges: the Viaduc de Martrou, which carries the modern road over the Charente, and its more unusual transporter bridge predecessor. After 5.2km, when the track has almost reached the D733, turn right over a wooden bridge. Follow the trail back to the river, passing under the viaduct and reaching the **Pont Transbordeur** after 1.5km.

The **Pont Transbordeur Rochefort-Martrou** opened in 1900 and could carry up to 14 tonnes across the Charente on a platform suspended by steel cables from 66m-high towers.

In 1966, the bridge featured in the French musical-comedy film *Les Demoiselles de Rochefort*, now available free online. If you watch the opening credits, you may want to slip on your white ankle boots and dance away the 75 seconds that the bridge takes to complete its 175m crossing.

The bridge was abandoned a year after the film was made and remained unused until its restoration in 1994. It is now one of only eight transporter bridges in the world still operating and is open for passengers from the end of March to the beginning of November.

Continue on the track along the river for 4.5km, crossing the entrances to numerous historic dockyards, before arriving at the Écluse du Bassin du Commerce, in **Rochefort** (**50km, 2hr 35min**).

ROCHEFORT

Rochefort was established in 1665 when the Catholic Louis XIV wanted a new naval base on the Atlantic as he could no longer rely on the Protestant-controlled port at La Rochelle. The original town plan, a grid of straight streets and a large central square, is still evident today.

The king's steward responsible for the building of the town between 1688 and 1710 was Michel Bégon; also a keen botanist, he gave his name to the Begonia, which became the first plant species to be named after a person. The Conservatoire du Bégonia has the largest collection of Begonias in the world and is open to the public from February to November.

The solid 17th-century architecture that Bégon oversaw still dominates the town. The recently restored Corderie Royale (Royal Rope Factory) was built in 1670 and, at over 370m long, was for centuries the longest manufacturing building in the world. The Rochefort Arsenal with its monumental gateway is now home to the National Navy Museum. Rochefort remained primarily a garrison town until it was decommissioned in 1926, when the tourist industry, which had long existed due to the town's spa, grew in importance.

STAGE 13

Rochefort to Royan

Start	Rochefort, Écluse du Bassin du Commerce
Finish	Royan ferry port
Time	4hr 40min
Distance	83.7km
Ascent	260m
Descent	260m
Refreshments en route	Saint-Agnant, Marennes, Ronce-les-Bains, La Palmyre
Accommodation en route	Marennes, Ronce-les-Bains

Leaving Rochefort along the banks of the Charente, the stage then weaves its way through the salt marshes around Marennes and crosses the Seudre estuary. The scent of pine forests mingles with the salty air as you follow the coast to the lighthouse at La Coubre. Elegant Belle Époque villas then begin to line the route as you approach the end of the stage at the historic town of Royan.

From the Bassin du Commerce, take the cycle path that follows the bank of the Charente, upstream for 750m. Turn left before a large car park, then turn right alongside the Avenue du Colonel Fuller. Follow the cycle lane for 4.2km, passing over the Canal de la Daurade and next two roundabouts before arriving at a smaller roundabout in front of Église Saint-Étienne in **Tonnay-Charente**. Turn right onto Rue de l'Église and follow for 200m to rejoin the river.

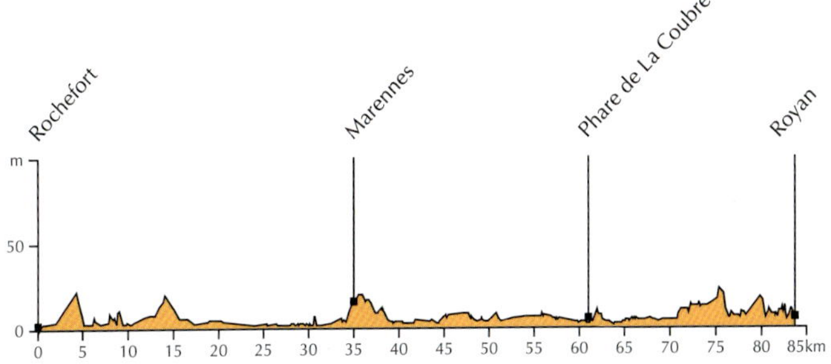

Crossing over the Canal de la Seudre à la Charente

Turn left and follow the Charente for 1.1km, passing underneath the historic suspension bridge and in front of the elegant Château des Capucins, to a bend in the road. Follow the road away from the river for 300m. Turn right onto a lane before the railway bridge. Continue under the road bridge to reach a T-junction after 1.5km. Turn left over the level crossing, then right onto Rue Lucien Lamothe and follow for 500m to a T-junction. Turn right, alongside the park with a lake, and follow for 600m to a T-junction in **Cabariot** (**9.1km, 30min**).

Turn right onto Rue des Gabares. After 600m, go over the level crossing and in 200m, turn right towards the Pont de la Cèpe, then bear left to join the cycle track along the old railway. There now follows 10km of delightful cycling along the course of the old railway, crossing the Charente via the old railway bridge and then running alongside the Canal de la Charente à la Seudre to the old station at **Saint-Agnant** (**20.3km, 1hr 5min**).

Continue on the cycle track, passing under the D733 road bridge, for 5km to **Bellevue**, where two canals intersect at a sluice. Cross over the sluice bridge and continue along the opposite bank of the Seudre à la Charente canal for 1.1km.

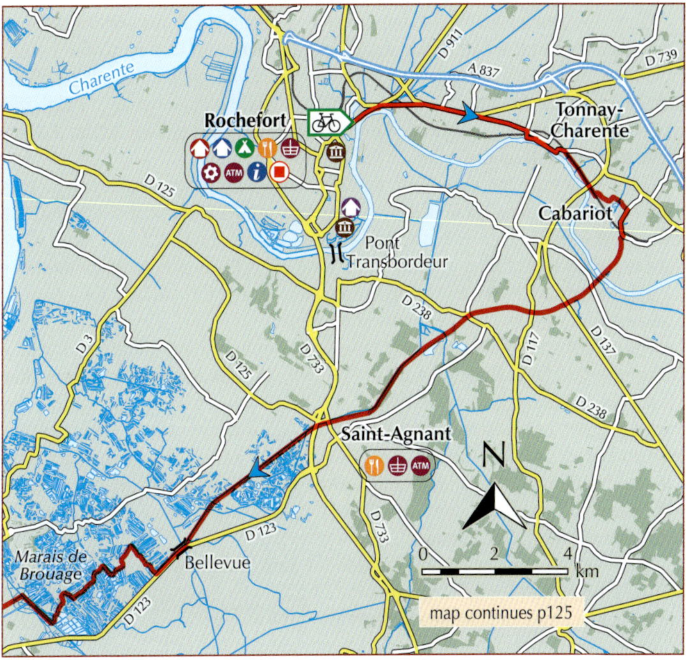

map continues p125

Turn right and follow the cycle track as it twists its way through the Marais de Brouage for 5km before rejoining the canal at a T-junction. Turn right, then follow the straight lane for 1.1km to a T-junction. Turn left, cross over the canal, then follow another straight lane for another 1.1km to another T-junction. Turn left, then after 100m, at the end of the woodland, turn right. Follow the lane for 400m, then turn right and follow Fief de Jean Roy for 1.1km to a T-junction on the outskirts of **Marennes** (**35.2km, 1hr 55min**).

Pretty cottages in Marennes-Hiers-Brouage

Turn right, then take the first left onto Rue du Petit Breuil. Turn right at the no-entry sign, then at the end of the short lane, turn left onto Rue du Grand Breuil. When the road bends right, turn left onto Rue Goulbeneze then immediately right onto Rue des Sifflets. After 50m, turn left and follow the track between fields and woodland for 1km to a T-junction. Turn left and follow the track for 800m, passing **Château de la Gataudière**, to reach the Marennes bypass.

Turn right onto the cycle lane that runs alongside the road and follow to a large roundabout after 300m. Follow the cycle lanes at the roundabout to bear left towards Marennes Plage. Take the cycle lane alongside the D728 for 3.5km, passing a roundabout featuring a giant boy running along the beach, to the bridge over the **Seudre estuary**. Cross the bridge and continue on the cycle lane for 2.6km to a roundabout with giant paper boats in the centre.

Turn right and follow the cycle lane for 800m to a small roundabout with a tree in the middle at **Ronce-les-Bains** (**45.2km, 2hr 30min**). Bear left, then after 100m, the cycle track leaves the road and heads left into the trees. Follow the track for 2.5km until it starts to run parallel to the road. After 300m, cross over the road and head back into the forest. All along this section of meandering track, you can find beautiful, quiet sandy beaches just a short detour down any of the tracks that head off to your right. After 13.1km of tranquil cycling, you arrive at **Phare de la Coubre** (**61.1km, 3hr 25min**).

Turn left and follow the cycle track for 5km to the marina at **La Palmyre**. Follow the seafront for 1.7km before curving left at a headland reinforced with boulders to a sandy beach. Head inland along the Promenade de Deux Phares for 800m. Before the track meets the road, turn right and follow it through the forest and the dunes for 3.8km to a road junction.

Turn right onto Avenue de Palmyre for 900m to the beach at La Grande Côte. Turn left and follow the seafront for 3.1km to **Saint-Palais-sur-Mer**. Continue for 7km, passing many well-maintained carrelets and the Cockle Shell Heroes Memorial, to the ferry port in **Royan** (**83.7km, 4hr 40min**).

In December 1942, **Operation Frankton** saw a British submarine surface in the Atlantic, 16km from the mouth of the Gironde estuary. Five canvas kayaks were launched and ten British Royal Marines set off to paddle the 96km along the Gironde to the German-occupied port of Bordeaux. Their plan was to attach limpet mines to docked ships and then escape overland to Spain.

Only two of the marines survived, Herbert Hasler, the commanding officer, and Bill Sparks. Of the other eight, six were executed by the Germans and two died from hypothermia. Two German vessels were sunk and four were damaged. In 1955, a heavily fictionalised film, *The Cockleshell Heroes*, immortalised the bravery of the marines. A monument

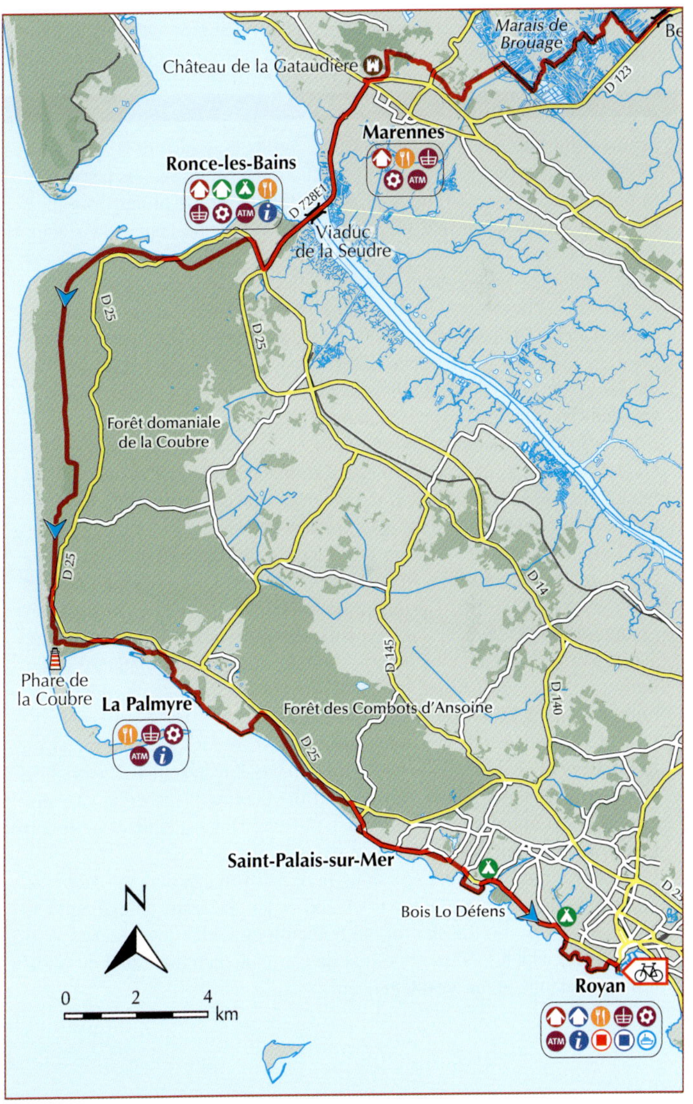
Marais de Brouage
Château de la Gataudière
D 123
Marennes
Ronce-les-Bains
D 728E1
Viaduc de la Seudre
D 25
D 25
Forêt domaniale de la Coubre
D 25
D 14
D 145
D 140
Phare de la Coubre
La Palmyre
Forêt des Combots d'Ansoine
D 25
Saint-Palais-sur-Mer
Bois Lo Défens
Royan
N
0
2
4
km

commemorating their sacrifice stands beside La Vélodyssée, overlooking the mouth of the Gironde.

ROYAN

Royan sits at the mouth of the Gironde and its long history is a cycle of fortification, prosperity, siege and destruction. The peninsula was first settled in prehistoric times, and the Romans built villas on the profits from their vineyards, oyster farms and salt production. In the fifth century, Visigoths arrived and built defensive walls around Royan, but these were insufficient in preventing the Vikings from plundering the town centuries later.

In 1154, Royan came under English control when Eleanor of Aquitaine married Henry Plantagenet (soon Henry II), and they set about fortifying the town. In 1355, the Black Prince further strengthened Royan's defences, but all was again to no avail. By the end of the Hundred Years' War, the town was French again and Royan was in ruins.

Royan slowly began to prosper once again, and after the signing of the Edict of Nantes, it became a Protestant stronghold until it was besieged by the Catholic King Louis XIII and the town was forced to surrender. In 1631, Cardinal Richelieu ordered the levelling of the town and its fortifications.

In the 19th century, during the Bourbon Restoration, and especially during the Second Empire, Royan was celebrated for its sea-bathing and it attracted many artists. During La Belle Époque, it saw the construction of fantastical seaside villas and magnificent boulevards. At the outbreak of World War 2, the Germans heavily fortified Royan, and in January 1945, during a raid by 350 Allied bombers, Royan was once again reduced to ruins, becoming known as the martyred city.

After World War 2, Royan became a showcase for Modernist architecture and is now considered to be the most 'fifties' city in France. The brightly coloured shops and apartments around the curving Plage de la Grande-Conche, the Central Market, the church of Notre-Dame and the Convention Centre all represent this architectural style.

Today, Royan is a thriving fishing port, and you can dine in one of the unpretentious cafés around the dock and watch the boats unloading their catch. Royan is also the start of the 800km-long Canal des 2 Mers à Vélo cycle route, which follows the Canal de Garonne then the Canal du Midi, from the Atlantic to the Mediterranean.

AQUITAINE

Cycling through the forest, approaching Lacanau-Océan (Stage 14)

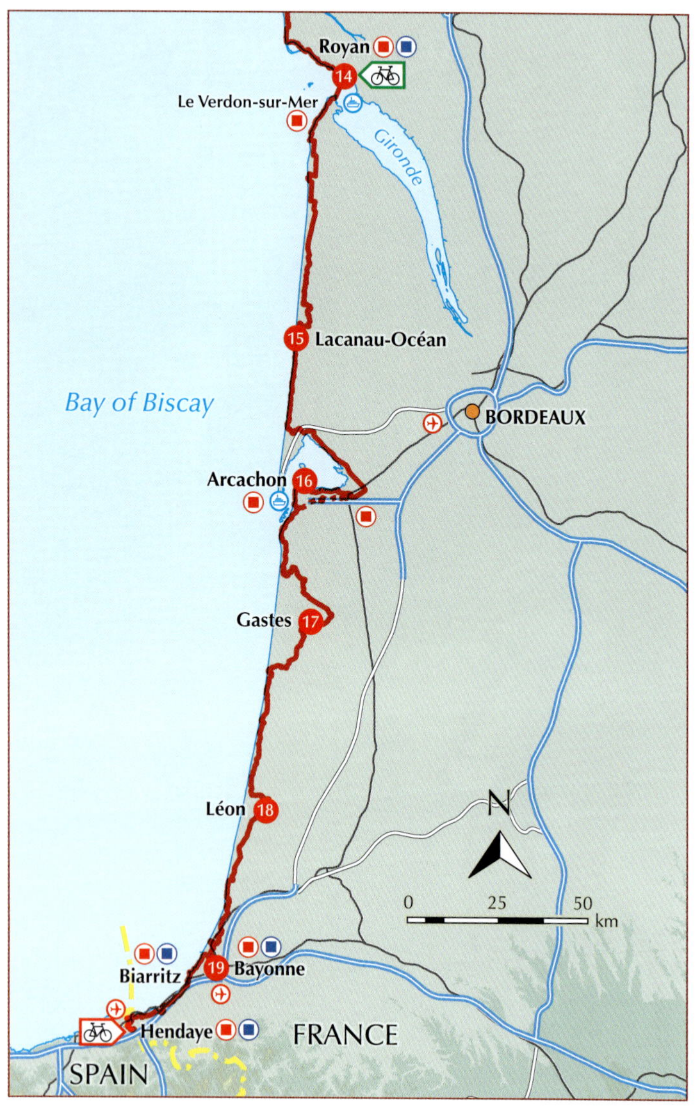
Royan
14
Le Verdon-sur-Mer
Gironde
15
Lacanau-Océan
Bay of Biscay
BORDEAUX
Arcachon
16
Gastes
17
Léon
18
N
0
25
50
km
Biarritz
19
Bayonne
Hendaye
FRANCE
SPAIN

STAGE 14

Royan to Lacanau-Océan

Start	Royan ferry port
Finish	Lacanau-Océan, Place du Général de Gaulle
Time	4hr 40min
Distance	84.3km
Ascent	260m
Descent	250m
Refreshments en route	Plage du Gurp, Montalivet-les-Bains, Plage du Pin Sec, Hourtin Plage, Carcans Plage and Maubuisson
Accommodation en route	Plage du Gurp, Montalivet-les-Bains, Plage du Pin Sec, Hourtin Plage, Carcans Plage and Maubuisson

The stage starts by crossing the wide Gironde estuary. It then heads south along undulating forest tracks, with the sandy shore and crashing waves of the Atlantic Ocean never more than a few hundred metres to your right. Beachside holiday towns provide opportunities for refreshment between sections of joyous forest cycling.

Take the ferry across the Gironde from Royan to **Le Verdon-sur-Mer**. You have now left the department of Charente-Maritim, and are in Gironde, in the region of Aquitaine.

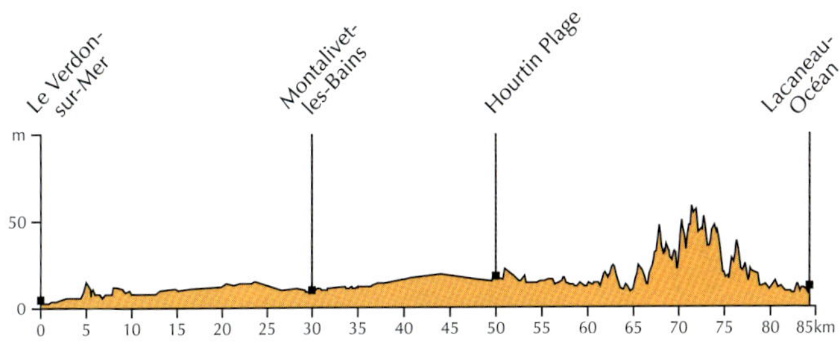

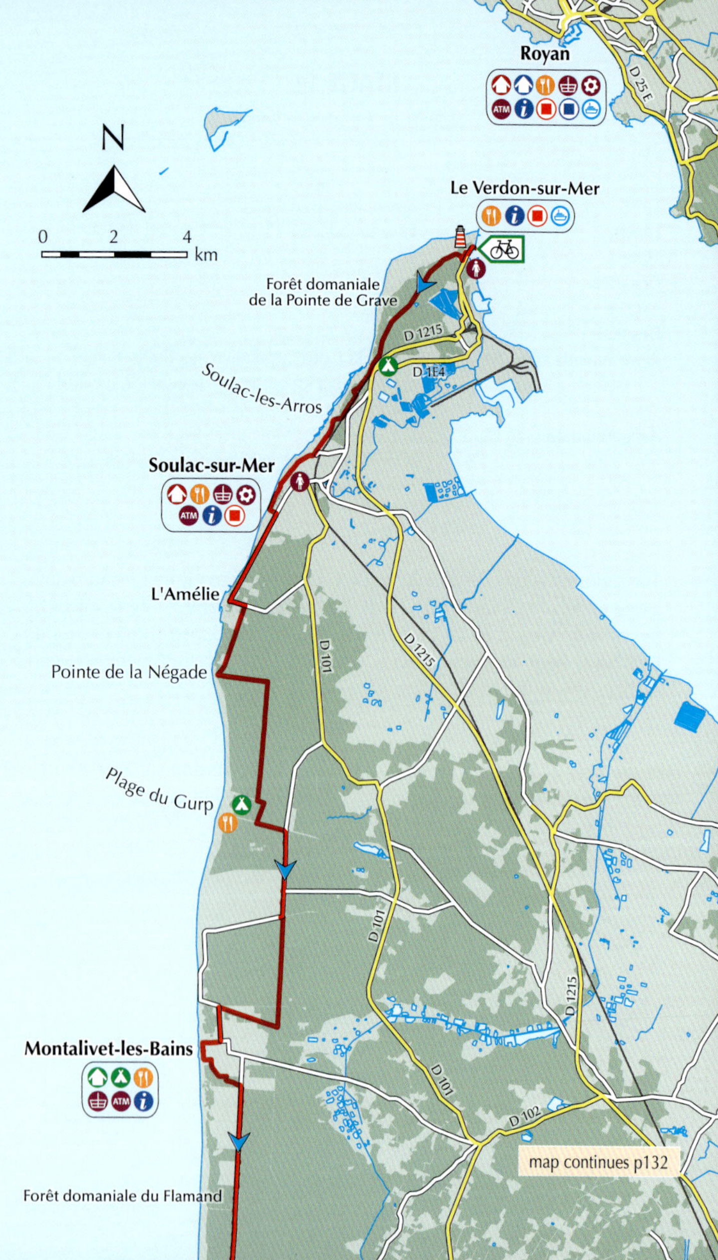

map continues p132

In July and August, the **Gironde ferry** operates on a continuous rotation. The 7km crossing takes about 30min; the first sailing is at 07:15 and the last at 20:00. It costs about €5 for an adult, with reductions for children and low-season crossings. No booking is needed, and bikes are carried at no extra charge. The shortest alternative land journey from Royan to Le Verdon-sur-Mer is 233km.

Disembark from the ferry and cycle past the tourist information office. Take your first right onto Allée du Sémaphore, then turn left at the red buoy by the lighthouse onto Cité des Douanes. Turn right by the trainlines for the PGVS tourist train and follow the lane for 100m to where the road forks by a row of garages. Cross the trainlines and follow the excellent cycle track that runs alongside them for 6.4km to **Soulac-les-Arros**, which has an abundance of picnic tables (**8.4km, 30min**).

The route now runs along the seafront promenade at **Soulac-sur-Mer** for 2.7km, with pavement cafés and a white sandy beach lining the route. At the end of the promenade, the cycle lane heads inland for 200m, then turns right alongside Boulevard de l'Amélie and follows it for 2.7km to the beach at **L'Amélie** (**12.7km, 40min**).

This section of the coast is littered with the remains of **World War 2** concrete bunkers; some are next to the cycle track and some, like those at L'Amélie, are gradually disappearing into the sandy beach.

Turn left at the red-and-white church, then turn right after 500m and follow the cycle lane for 2km to the beach at **Pointe de la Négade**. Turn left, then after 1.4km, turn right onto a track that leads through the forest for 3.9km to **Plage du Gurp** (**20.4km, 1hr 5min**).

Family on tour at Montalivet-les-Bains

Turn left, then after 800m, turn right at the roundabout and follow the straight cycle track for 5.4km. Turn right, then after 1.7km, turn left onto a lane between two campsites. Follow the lane for 900m, then turn right onto the cycle path alongside Boulevard Général Leclerc and follow for 900m to the beach at **Montalivet-les-Bains** (**29.7km, 1hr 40min**).

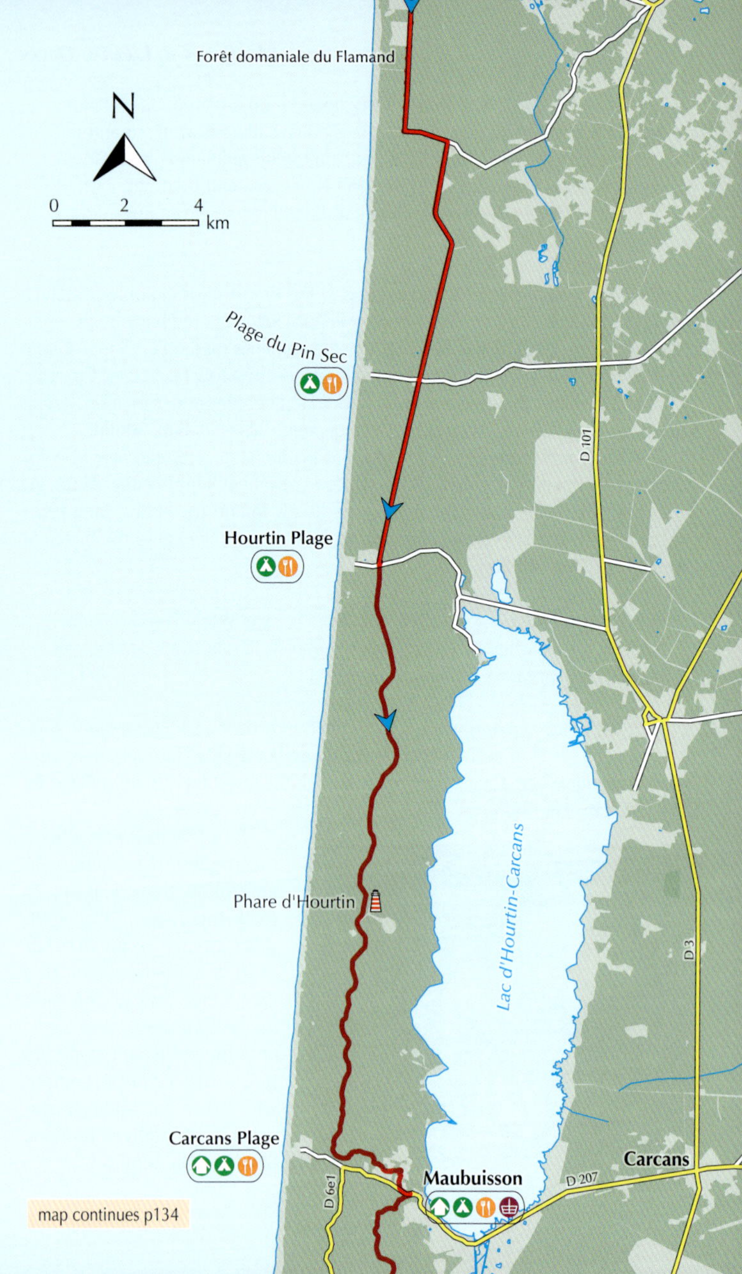

map continues p134

Whale-tail sculpture on the beach at Plage de Montalivet

Head along the seafront for 400m until Boulevard du Front de Mer turns left. Turn right onto a cycle track, which soon curves left. After 300m, at the end of the car park, follow the track round to the right and alongside Rue de Grand Bretagne for 600m. Just after the road bears to the left, turn right into a height-restricted car park, then turn left onto a cycle track. Follow the track through the trees for 600m until it reaches the Avenue de l'Europe.

Turn right and follow the cycle track that runs alongside the road for 5.2km. When the road turns left, continue to follow it for another 1.2km, then turn right. Follow the cycle lane alongside the road for 6.6km to the crossroads with Route du Pin Sec (**44.6km, 2hr 30min**). Cross the road and continue for 5.1km to the crossroads with Route de Contaut at **Hourtin Plage** (**49.7km, 2hr 45min**).

Head straight across the road onto Route des Phares and follow it through the Forêt d'Hourtin for 9.7km to a lighthouse, the Phare d'Hourtin. Continue for 7.1km through the dunes and pine forest, between the large Lac d'Hourtin-Carcans and the Atlantic Ocean, to a crossroads of tracks (**66.5km, 3hr 40min**).

The right turn at this crossroads leads to the beach and cafés of Carcans Plage, but the route turns left and continues through the forest for 3.3km. Just before the track meets the roundabout on the D207, there is a cycle-track junction. Straight ahead at this roundabout leads to the sandy beach, campsite and lakeside cafés at **Maubuisson**. The route turns right, crosses over the road and heads back into the forest.

Follow the well-surfaced track for 6km as it undulates like a gentle roller coaster through the sandy forest to a crossroad of tracks. Turn right and follow the track for

1.9km to a crossroads with the D6E1. Cross the road and continue along the asphalted cycle track for 1.2km to a crossroads of tracks in a clearing with a derelict building. Turn left and follow the track through the forest for 3.7km to a T-junction with Avenue du Cantabria. Cross the road, turn left and take the cycle track that runs beside the road for 900m. At the junction of cycle tracks next to Avenue Raoul Plantey, the waymarked route turns left to follow a cycle track that circles around the town. Turn right and follow the cycle track for 900m to the Place du Général de Gaulle, in the centre of **Lacaneau-Océan** (**84.3km, 4hr 40min**).

Cycling through the forest of the Étang de Cousseau nature reserve

LACANEAU-OCÉAN

Lacaneau-Océan's promenade is a mixture of villas built in the first half of the 20th century and apartments built in the second. The very long sandy beach is popular with families, surfers and young holidaymakers. It offers plenty of affordable accommodation and places to eat to suit most tastes.

STAGE 15

Lacanau-Océan to Arcachon

Start	Lacanau-Océan, Place du Général de Gaulle
Finish	Arcachon, Jetée Thiers
Time	4hr
Distance	80.1km
Ascent	130m
Descent	140m
Variant route	Waymarked La Vélodyssée route bypassing Arcachon (18.5km, +70m/-30m, 1hr)
Refreshments en route	Le Porge-Océan, Le Grand Crohot, Andernos-les-Bains, Audenge and Biganos
Accommodation en route	Le Porge-Océan, Le Grand Crohot, Andernos-les-Bains and Biganos

The stage starts by following well-surfaced paths through the tranquil forest, only interrupted by opportunities for refreshment at the wild beaches of Le Porge-Océan and Le Grand Crohot. It then heads inland before joining a voie verte along a disused railway line and then cycle paths around Arcachon Bay to the genteel seaside resort of Arcachon.

From the roundabout in the Place du Général de Gaulle, head south along Rue Gabriel Dupuy for 500m to a roundabout, then bear left onto Route du Lion, towards Plage Sud. Follow the lane for 600m, then turn left onto a cycle track, opposite a public toilet. Go straight across at the cycle track crossroads and

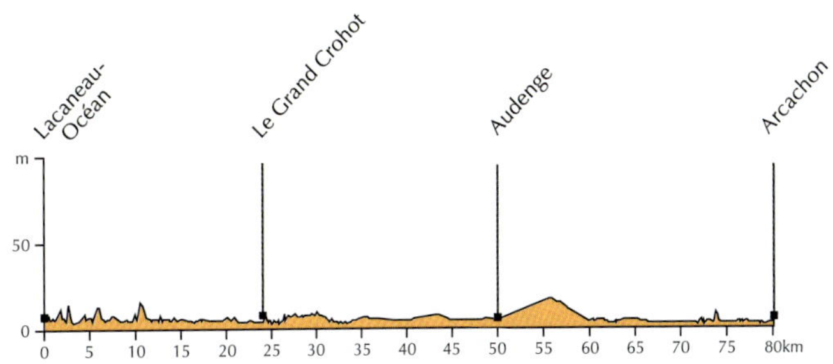

map continues p139

continue for 12km to the restaurants, campsite, large car park and fantastic sandy beach at **Le Porge-Océan** (**13km, 40min**).

The route continues 11.3km through the forest, close to the ocean and passing the popular naturist beach at La Jenny, to the restaurants, campsite, large car park and another excellent beach, at **Le Grand Crohot** (**24.3km, 1hr 15min**).

Continue on the well-surfaced cycle path for 1.5km to a fork in the track, bear left, then after 4.7km, at another fork in the track, bear right. Continue for 2km until the track meets Route du Cap Ferret. Turn left just before the road and follow the track that runs adjacent to the D106 for 2.7km, passing a roundabout and crossing a canal and two slip-roads onto D106, to a T-junction of two cycle tracks. Turn right and pass under the D106. Follow the voie verte along a disused railway for 1.2km to a roundabout in **Arès** (**36.5km, 1hr 50min**).

Go straight ahead for 4km to the former station in **Andernos-les-Bains**, which now hosts the tourist information office. Continue for 6.8km to the old station building in Lanton, then continue for a further 2.9km to the disused station in **Audenge**. Follow the voie verte for its final 6.4km to where the disused railway meets the used railway at Avenue de la Côte d'Argent in **Biganos** (**56.6km, 2hr 50min**).

Turn right and follow the cycle track alongside the road for 4.7km. After passing over the river Eyre, and just before the roundabout, follow the cycle path to the right. Continue for 1.4km to a road junction, where Rue de Stade meets Rue du Pont Neuf to the right and Rue de Jeangard to the left.

The waymarked route of La Vélodyssée now avoids Arcachon by turning left and following the **route variant** (see route description below), joining Stage 16 near Dune du Pilat. This reduces the combined distance for Stages 15 and 16 by 9.2km but misses out pleasant cycling along the seafront in the elegant town of Arcachon. If choosing to follow the variant, you could shorten Stage 15 by finishing it at Biganos, making Stages 15 and 16 55km and 80km, respectively, or alternatively you could extend Stage 15 to finish at Dune du Pilat, making the two stages 80km and 55km, respectively.

For the next 27.7km, the route follows COBAS 1, itinéraire côtier, waymarked by La Communauté d'Agglomération du Bassin d'Arcachon Sud; look for the circular blue signs bearing a white number 1. Turn right onto Rue du Pont Neuf and follow for 100m, then turn left by the electricity substation and follow the cycle path for 200m to Rue Saint-Louis. Turn left, then right at the T-junction, towards the church, and go straight across the roundabout in front of the Mairie. At L'Église Saint-André, by the large market square in **Le Teich**, turn left onto the cycle path that runs alongside Avenue de la Gare and follow this for 500m to the roundabout by the bike shop. Turn right, go past the railway station and follow Rue de

The pier and beach at Arcachon

l'Industrie for 400m to a T-junction. Turn left, go over the level crossing, then turn right onto Avenue de Camps.

Follow the road for 800m, then just after a crossroads, leave the cycle track and bear right onto Rue de Matato. After 1.2km, at the T-junction, turn right onto Allée du Haurat and follow the cycle lane for 700m, going straight across at the roundabout to the railway line. Go over the level crossing and turn left. Follow the cycle lane between the railway and the waterfront for 1.4km to the railway station at **Gujan-Mestras** (**68.2km, 3hr 25min**).

Continue for 3.6km to a T-junction in **Port de la Hume**. Turn left onto the cycle path on Avenue de la Plage, go over the level crossing and then turn immediately right onto a cycle path. Follow the cycle path alongside the D650 for 2.7km to the roundabout by the port and railway station in **La Teste**.

Bear right at the roundabout, keeping the harbour on your right, and follow Avenue du Général Leclerc for 2.6km to the roundabout junction with Boulevard Deganne. Turn right onto Boulevard Pierre Loti, then take your first left at the small roundabout onto Rue Coste. Follow for 300m to the sea. Turn left and follow the waterfront, passing the yacht marina and following the wide, flat north shore boarding along the beach for 2km to the Jetée Thiers in **Arcachon** (**80.1km, 4hr**).

ARCACHON

Until the middle of the 19th century, Arcachon was a forest of pines and oaks on the sandy shore of a tidal basin. It had no road links, few buildings and a population of fewer than 400. In 1857, Napoleon III declared Arcachon an autonomous municipality and the railway line arrived, and so the seaside resort was born. The style of seaside villas that flourished is now known as Arcachonnaise, with one of the most famous being the elegant Villa Alexandre Dumas. Built in 1895, it is named after the author of *The Three Musketeers* even though he never stayed there. In fact, Alexandre Dumas visited Arcachon only once, for a week, 30 years before work was started on the villa.

Unveiled in 1948, the statue of Heracles in the Parc Mauresque commemorates the sacrifices of French Resistance fighters in World War 2. The nude statue has been vandalised so frequently that in 2016 the Arcachon

Whale-tail sculpture at Arcachon

authorities installed a removable penis, only temporarily remounting it for special occasions.

There is an air of gentility and civic pride about the town, with its long promenade, piers, vintage carousel and sculpture of a whale's tail that appears just off the shoreline. The town, with its calm sheltered bathing accessed from shallow sandy beaches, is popular with young families.

Variant: Le Teich to Dune du Pilat roundabout (joining Stage 16)

Turn left and follow Rue de Jeangard for 300m to a roundabout. Go straight across and continue for 1.1km, passing over a level crossing, to another roundabout. Turn right onto Avenue François Mitterrand and follow for 900m to a roundabout with trees on it. Bear left towards the large water tower, then after 200m, bear right onto the cycle path that runs next to it. After 500m the track meets Rue de la Mission. Turn right and follow the cycle lane for 2.8km to a roundabout next to an apartment block with a large archway. Turn left, then after 200m, cross the road and follow the cycle path over a bridge beneath the trees. Follow for 3km to Route des Lacs in **La Teste-de-Buch**.

Turn left then follow the track alongside the road for 500m, passing the big slide in the waterpark. Cross the road before the roundabout then double back on yourself. Take the cycle path that heads left away from the road and then runs adjacent to the N250 for 4.3km to the junction with Rue Jean Larrieu.

Turn left, pass underneath the N250, then turn right onto a cycle path. Follow the cycle path next to the D259 for 4.6km to a large roundabout at the **Dune du Pilat**, rejoining La Vélodyssée waymarked route 10.2km into Stage 16 (**18.5km, 1hr** after leaving main route at Le Teich.

STAGE 16

Arcachon to Gastes

Start	Arcachon, Jetée Thiers
Finish	Mimizan Plage, Pont du Courant de Mimizan
Time	3hr 35min
Distance	66.2km
Ascent	300m
Descent	280m
Refreshments en route	Dune du Pilat, Biscarrosse Plage, Navarrosse, Biscarrosse and Parentis-en-Born
Accommodation en route	Dune du Pilat, Biscarrosse Plage, Navarrosse, Biscarrosse and Parentis-en-Born

A shorter stage than recent days, the route offers plenty of places for refreshment stops along the way. Leaving Arcachon along the shore, between elegant villas and sandy beaches, it heads to the massive sand dune at Pilat. You can walk up the dune, although it is a very busy tourist attraction, popular with coach parties in the summer. A good view of the dune can be had looking back from further along the stage. A gentle climb leads to the high road overlooking the dunes before descending through forest tracks to rejoin the coast. Leaving the Atlantic behind, the route meanders along woodland paths around two inland lakes to the quiet waters, and sandy beach at Gastes.

From Jetée Thiers, head west along the beachfront cycle path for 600m to the T-junction with Boulevard de la Plage. Take the cycle path round to the right and then continue for 500m to Jetée de La Chapelle. Follow the delightful

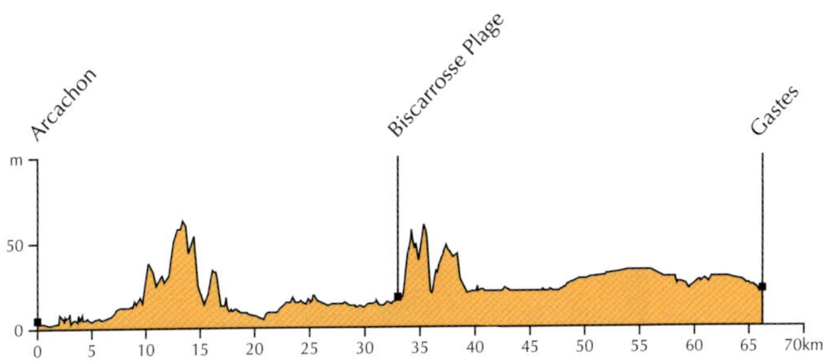

Arcachon railway station

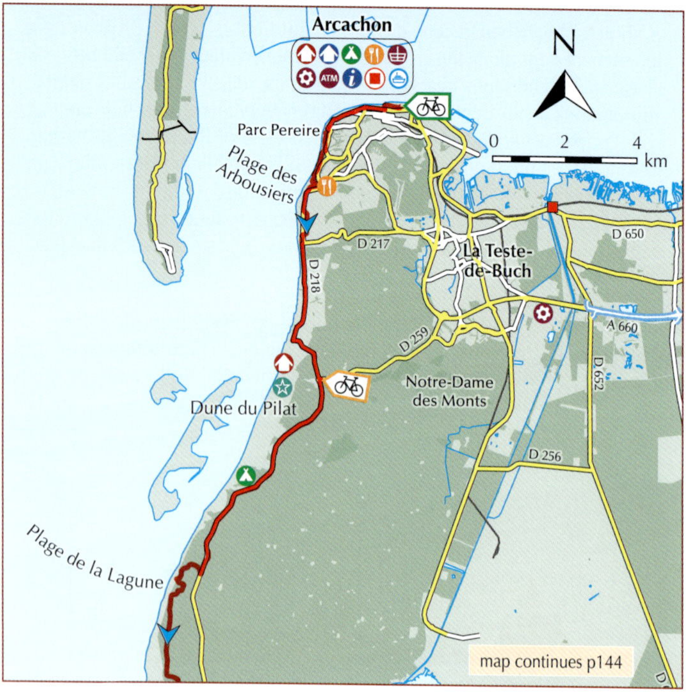

Arcachon
N
0 2 4 km
Parc Pereire
Plage des Arbousiers
D 217
D 218
La Teste-de-Buch
D 650
A 660
D 259
D 652
Notre-Dame des Monts
Dune du Pilat
D 256
Plage de la Lagune

map continues p144

beachfront cycle path for 2.8km, alongside Boulevard de l'Océan and Plage Pereire, to **Plage des Arbousiers**.

The track starts to head inland and then runs parallel to the coast for 4.7km to a roundabout with a single olive tree in the middle. Bear left and follow the cycle lane along Avenue de Biscarrosse for 1.4km to the large, wooded roundabout at **Dune du Pilat**, where you rejoin the waymarked route of La Vélodyssée (**10.2km, 35min**).

The **Dune du Pilat** rises 107m above sea level, making it the tallest sand dune in Europe. It is 500m wide and 2.7km long, and it is made up of 60,000,000m^3 of sand. In 2013, a tourist found an Iron Age funeral urn at the foot of the dune, which suggests it has been an important site for visitors for millennia. It now receives more than two million visitors per year, with most coming in the summer months. Due to its exposed location along the sea and its steep angle, the dune is a popular venue for paragliding.

La Dune du Pilat

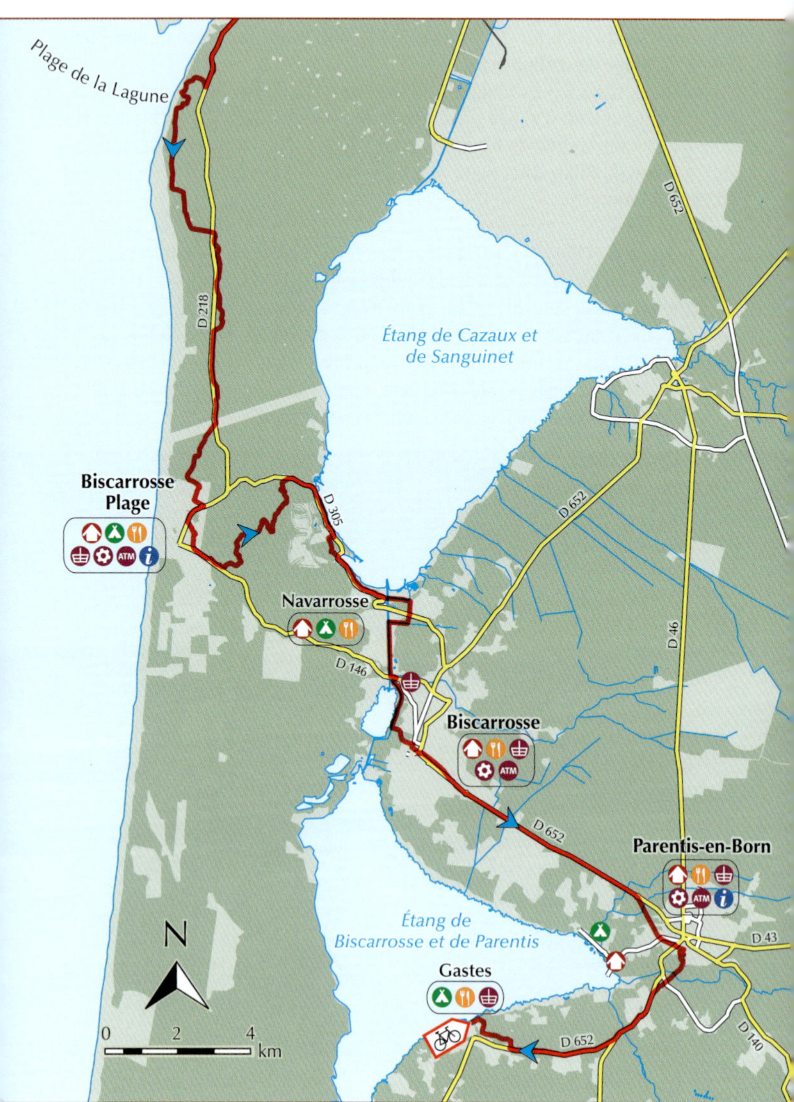

Plage de la Lagune
D 218
Étang de Cazaux et de Sanguinet
D 652
Biscarrosse Plage
D 305
D 652
Navarrosse
D 146
D 46
Biscarrosse
D 652
Parentis-en-Born
Étang de Biscarrosse et de Parentis
D 43
Gastes
N
0
2
4
km
D 652
D 140
ATM

Continue straight across at the roundabout to the cycle track on the left-hand side of the D218 and follow for 6.7km. Initially, you experience something rarely felt since leaving Brittany – an incline. As the road rises from the roundabout, you can look back at the Dune du Pilat and, on most days, see the solid line of visitors walking to the top of the dune.

Soon after passing the large car park and campsites at Le Petit Nice, the cycle track crosses over the road and descends through the pine forest on a well-surfaced track for 1.5km to reach the beach car park and public toilets at **La Lagune** (**18.4km, 1hr**). Cross the road and continue along the excellent path for 2.3km to La Salie Nord. After the car park, the track heads inland for 2km, back to the D128.

Cross the road and follow the track that runs through the forest parallel to it for 5.5km. Cross back over the road and follow the path for 2.1km until it arrives at Rue du Tit. Turn right and continue for 400m to a roundabout, then turn left and reach another roundabout after 300m. Turn right onto Avenue du Pyla, then after 600m, bear left. Follow Avenue du Clair de Lune for 900m to the roundabout at the junction with Avenue de la Plage in **Biscarrosse Plage** (**32.5km, 1hr 45min**).

Bear left onto the cycle track, which soon leaves the road and undulates through forest-covered sand dunes for 6.4km to the beach on the inland lake of Étang de Cazaux et de Sanguinet at Maguide. Follow the lakeside cycle path for 4.7km to the canal and campsites at **Navarrosse**. At the end of the canal, turn right onto a cycle lane and follow for 600m, then turn right and continue for 500m to where the path joins the bank of the canal.

Turn left and follow the canal for 1.4km to Avenue de Laouadie. Cross the road and continue along the canal for 1.7km to where the path turns left. Follow the path for 1.1km to a roundabout by the old station in **Biscarrosse** (**48.8km, 2hr 35min**).

Join the cycle track along the course of the old railway, pass the old station building and continue for 1.4km until you meet Avenue du Maréchal Lyautey. Cross the road and follow the cycle path that runs alongside it for 5.8km to a wooded roundabout. Bear right onto a disused railway cycle path and follow it for 1.8km to a roundabout by a supermarket in **Parentis-en-Born** (**57.8km, 3hr 5min**).

Continue straight ahead at the roundabout for 300m and then turn right 200m before the water tower. The cycle path soon leaves the town behind, crossing a wooden bridge over a small river and a quiet lane and then running alongside the D652 before arriving at a roundabout after 2.4km. Continue straight ahead, following the cycle path alongside the road for 1km to a fork in the road. Continue for 3.1km to where the path turns right and runs alongside the quiet Rue de Campet.

Essential end-of-day chores when cycle camping in the French summer

After 100m, turn left and follow the cycle path through the trees for 900m to a no-entry sign at a crossroad with a quiet lane. Turn right onto Avenue Jean Darmuzey, then after 300m, take the cycle path on your left, next to some wooden outdoor gym equipment. Follow the track for 400m to a roundabout by a sandy beach at **Gastes** (**66.3km, 3hr 35min**).

STAGE 17

Gastes to Léon

Start	Gastes beach
Finish	Léon, town square
Time	4hr
Distance	70.4km
Ascent	250m
Descent	250m
Refreshments en route	Sainte-Eulalie-en-Born, Mimizan Plage, Contis Plage, Cap de l'Homy and Saint-Girons-Plage
Accommodation en route	Sainte-Eulalie-en-Born, Mimizan Plage, Contis Plage, Cap de l'Homy and Saint-Girons-Plage

This stage follows the shores of two lakes before heading to the ocean. You then follow gently undulating, well-surfaced cycle paths through pine trees, with idyllic sandy beaches and the Atlantic always just a short detour to your right and a good choice of beachside cafés along the way. More forest tracks lead inland again to the lakeside town of Léon.

From the beach in Gastes, head west along the shore for a short distance. Before reaching the marina, cross over Avenue du Lac. Follow the lakeside for 3.1km to the beach, campsite and small marina at Plage Gaillard. Continue for 900m to the beach, campsite and smaller marina at the southern tip of the lake.

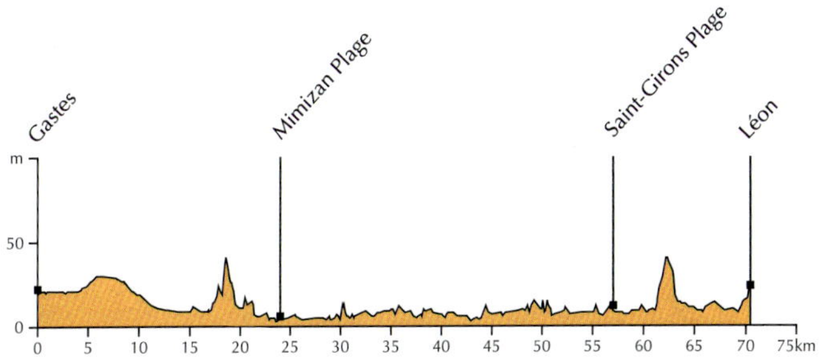

Étang de
Biscarrosse et de Parentis
Gastes
N
0
2
4
km
D 652
Sainte-Eulalie-en-Born
D 652
D 46
D 87
Étang
d'Aureilhan
Mimizan Plage
D 626
D 626
Arboretum
des Malgaches
Mimizan
D 44
D 652
D 652
D 38
Contis Plage
D 41
D 167
map continues p150
D 66

Head inland alongside Route du Lac for 1.9km. Follow the track as it turns right by the water tower and runs alongside Route de Parentis for 2.5km to **Sainte-Eulalie-en-Born**. Follow the cycle path through the town, along Rue du Lavoir then alongside Route Touristique, for 6.8km to a car park at Étang d'Aurelihan (**15.2km, 50min**).

Continue along the cycle path for 1.7km to the outskirts of **Mimizan**. Follow the cycle track as it turns right before the first house and continue for 4.8km through the pine forest to a junction of cycle paths and roads at Route des Plages Perdues.

Turn left, then after 300m, turn right onto Boulevard de l'Atlantique and follow for 1km to a roundabout. Bear left and follow Rue du Soleil Levant then Boulevard des Pêcheurs for 500m to reach the Pont du Courant de Mimizan in **Mimizan Plage** (**23.5km, 1hr 20min**).

Cross over the bridge and follow Rue des Lacs for 100m. Bear left onto the cycle path and follow for 1.3km to a junction of cycle paths. Turn right and follow the path alongside Route de Lespecier for 750m, then bear right and continue for 4.3km to the beach car park at Plage de Lespecier.

Cross the road, take the cycle track back into the pine forest and follow for 9.2km. Shortly after passing the Phare de Contis, you arrive at the beach and cafés in **Contis Plage** (**39.1km, 2hr 15min**).

Cycling in the forest near Cap de l'Homy

Turn left along Avenue de l'Océan and follow for 1km to the Pont Rose over the Courant de Contis. Cross over the bridge and take your first right onto Allée du Contour for 400m. Turn right onto Allée des Gourbets for 200m to where the cycle path heads off to the left.

Follow the cycle path through the forest for 5.9km to the Avenue de l'Océan at **Cap de l'Homy**. Cross over the road and continue along the cycle path through the forest for 3.4km to the natural spring at Yons (**50km, 2hr 40min**).

Continue on the cycle path through the forest for 6.6km to Route de la Plage at

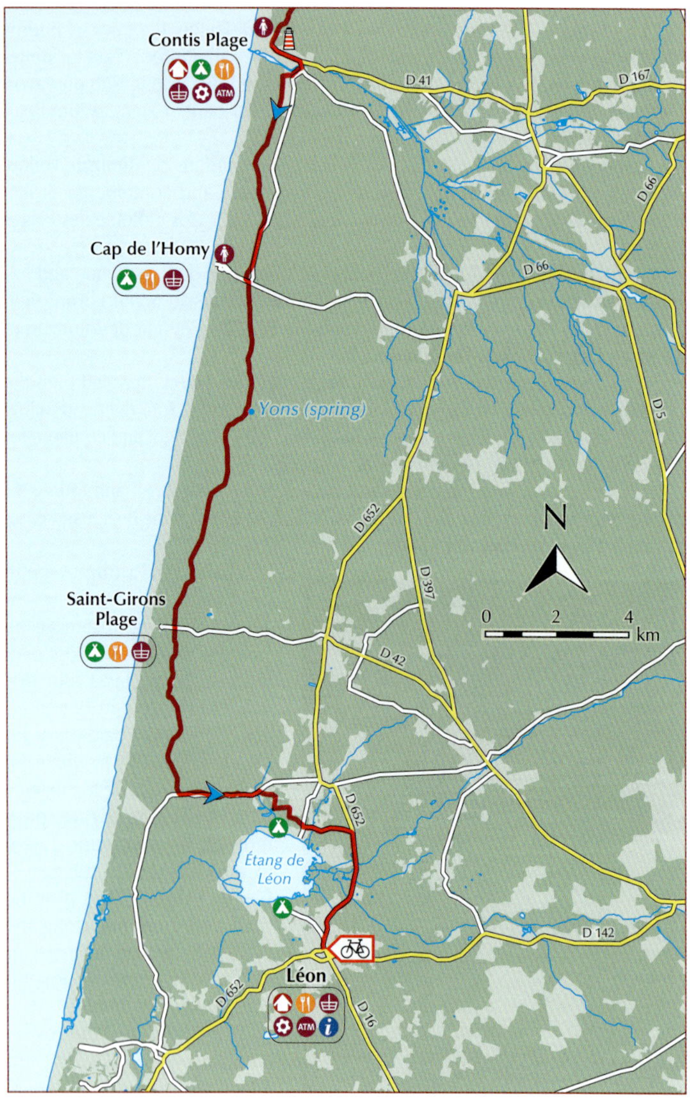
Contis Plage
ATM
D 41
D 167
D 66
Cap de l'Homy
D 66
Yons (spring)
D 5
D 652
N
D 397
Saint-Girons Plage
0
2
4
km
D 42
D 652
Étang de Léon
D 142
Léon
ATM
D 652
D 16

Saint-Girons-Plage. Cross the road and follow the cycle path for 4.7km to where the path forks before meeting the D328 (**61.3km, 3hr 30min**).

Turn left and follow the cycle path as it runs alongside Route de Pichelebe for 2.3km until it crosses over the road. Continue for 100m, then turn right and follow the cycle path for 500m until it meets Route de Bénédit. Turn right along the quiet lane for 400m, then turn left and follow the cycle path, crossing over the road twice and passing a picnic site, for 2.5km to a roundabout next to a campsite.

Turn right and follow Route des Lacs, initially on a cycle path and then along the road, for 2.9km to a small roundabout. Go straight ahead for 300m then continue straight across at an elliptical roundabout to the town square in **Léon** (**70.4km, 4hr**).

Camping in the forest at Vielle-Saint-Girons

STAGE 18

Léon to Bayonne

Start	Léon, town square
Finish	Bayonne, Place Charles de Gaulle
Time	3hr
Distance	61.9km
Ascent	130m
Descent	150m
Refreshments en route	Moliets-et-Maa, Messanges, Vieux-Boucau-les-Bains, Le Penon, Hossegor and Labenne-Océan
Accommodation en route	Moliets-et-Maa, Messanges, Vieux-Boucau-les-Bains, Le Penon, Hossegor and Labenne-Océan

This stage heads south, through pine forest and past sand dunes bordering world-class surfing beaches, to the historic, distinctly Basque city of Bayonne. If you can resist stopping at all of the fantastic beaches along the way, this relatively short stage gives you more time to explore the historic city of Bayonne.

From the town square in Léon, head south-east along Avenue Loys Labeque for 200m to a roundabout. Continue straight ahead, then turn right onto a cycle path along the course of an old railway. Follow the voie verte for 5.2km until it meets Rue de Cantegrouille by a picnic site at **Moliets-et-Maa**.

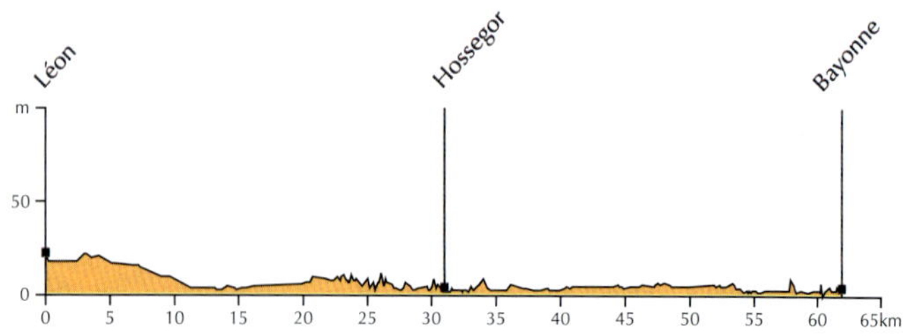

map continues p155

Follow the path for 3.9km to another picnic site, on Avenue du Coy in **Messanges**. Then continue for 4km to yet another picnic site, at the old railway station, now a private house, at **Vieux-Boucau-les-Bains** (**13.6km, 40min**).

Cycling between lakes near Métro

Surfing at Hossegor at sunset (photo: Jacob King)

Continue for 1.3km to a path on your right. Turn right, cross Route des Lacs, then turn left. Follow the path for 1.3km, over the Courrant de Soustons, to meet the D79. Cross the road and turn right onto the cycle path that runs adjacent to it for 7.2km to a wooded roundabout. Go straight ahead at the roundabout, then turn immediately right and cross the road to a picnic site with public toilets.

Follow the cycle path as it weaves between the picnic tables and then alongside the road. Continue for 4.3km, passing seven roundabouts, until you meet the sea at Avenue du Front de Mer in **Le Penon**. Turn right then follow the cycle path alongside the beachfront for 2.1km to Avenue de la Côte d'Argent. Follow the path to the left, then alongside the road for 800m to the **Pont d'Hossegor** (**30.7km, 1hr 30min**).

On a day in the height of the summer, when the Atlantic is serving little more than a ripple on the west coast beaches, it is hard to imagine that you are looking at a stop on the World Surf League world tour. However, Hossegor, with its best wave 'Le Gravier', is just that. Dubbed the **surfing capital of Europe**, Hossegor is world renowned for its heavy sand-bottomed barrelling beach-breaks. The waves are caused by storm systems in the North Atlantic; these generate swell that often meets favourable offshore easterly winds. Typically, the swell will start to arrive in early September.

The quality and consistency of the surf have given rise to a vibrant surf culture in Hossegor. The bike paths are populated with surfers riding fat-tired e-bikes fitted with surfboard racks, searching for uncrowded waves. In its surf shops, beach cafés and lively summer markets, the town of Hossegor confidently emits a surfing lifestyle vibe.

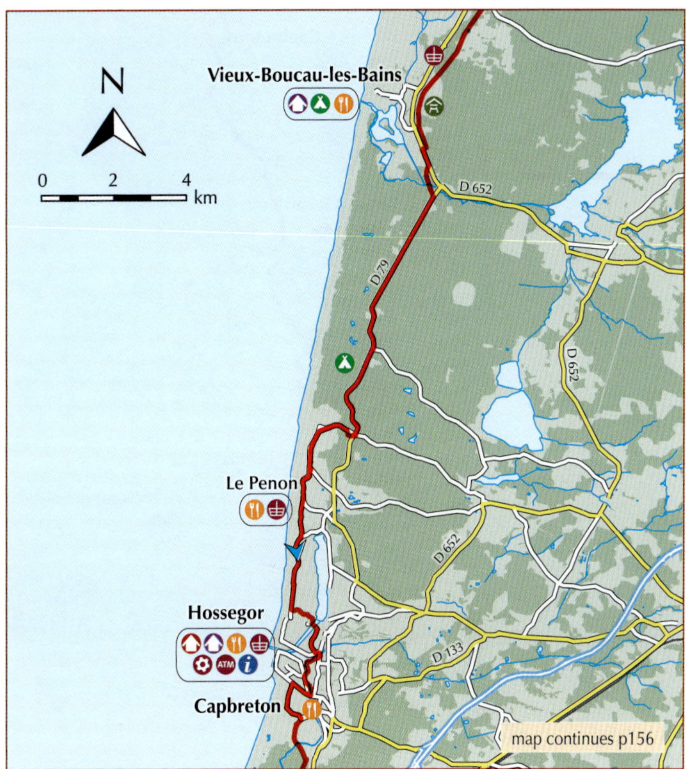

Cross the bridge, turn right and follow Avenue Brémontier for 700m to a roundabout. Go straight across onto a cycle path and follow it over the Canal du Bouret. Turn right and follow the quayside through the marina for 900m to the bridge over Le Boudigau.

Cross over the bridge, turn left and follow the west bank of the river for 600m to Pont Lajus in **Capbreton**. Turn right onto Avenue du Maréchal de Lattre de Tassigny and follow for 600m, passing the tourist information office, to the junction with Avenue de Biarritz. Turn left for 700m to the junction with Rue des Vignerons. Turn left, then after 600m, turn right onto Avenue des Alouettes.

After 200m, bear left onto a cycle path alongside Avenue de l'Adour and follow for 400m until it meets Rue de la Semie. Go straight across onto the cycle

track and follow it across the bridge over Le Boudigau, and alongside the boundary of a campsite, to a sharp right turn after 600m. Follow the cycle track for 800m to a crossroads. Turn right, then after 300m, turn left onto the cycle track alongside Le Boudigau. Follow the riverbank for 3.5km to the bridge at **Labenne-Océan** (**41km, 2hr 5min**).

Continue following the same bank of the river for 1.3km to a bridge. Turn right, cross the bridge and follow the track for 1.2km to the river L'Anguillère. Cross the bridge and continue for 800m to Avenue de la Plage. Turn right and follow the road for 400m to a roundabout. Turn left onto the cycle track and follow for 1.9km until it meets Chemin de la Bidassoa.

Cross the road and follow the cycle path between the road and the railway for 1.2km. Just after Chemin de la Bidassoa starts to run alongside the busier road at **Tarnos**, but before it reaches the roundabout, turn right onto a cycle track through the trees. After 2.2km the track arrives at a roundabout between the beach car park and a holiday park at **Plage du Métro** (**50km, 2hr 30min**).

Head inland, following Avenue Julian Grimau for 2.2km to the triangular Square Albert Mora. At the crossroads turn right onto Allée des Chasseurs, then after 100m, turn left onto Rue du 8 Mai 1945. After 300m, at the roundabout by the Salle des Fêtes, turn right onto Rue de Grives then at the mini roundabout by the tennis courts, turn left onto Rue de la Grande Baye.

Follow the road, bearing left by the skatepark, for 500m to Avenue Marcel Paul. Turn right, go straight ahead at the first roundabout, then after 500m, at a second roundabout, turn right. Cross over the old level crossing and turn left before the traffic lights onto Rue du Fronton. Cross over another old level crossing then bear left onto Rue des Forges, by the basketball court.

After 250m, turn right by the primary school onto Rue de la Cité, then bear left by **Église Notre-Dame-des-Forges** onto Rue Saint-Charles. At the T-junction with Rue Maurice Perse, turn left and follow the road for 200m to a level crossing. Cross over the railway lines, then bear right onto Rue Paul Biremont for 500m to **Boucau** railway station.

Continue following the road next to the railway for 2.8km. Just before the railway goes under the pink-sided road bridge, turn left onto a short section of cycle track, then turn right by the main road. Follow the cycle lane over the railway bridge to a roundabout after 300m. Turn right, then immediately cross the road and turn left on the cycle track, to head underneath the road bridge, on the bank of the river Adour.

Follow the quayside for 1.9km, passing under the historic Pont Saint-Esprit, until just before reaching the Pont Charles Vaillant railway bridge. Turn left onto Rue des Lavandières, then bear right onto the cycle path that leads up to the bridge.

Cross over the river, leaving behind the département of Landes and entering Pyrénées-Atlantiques. Turn right and follow the cycle path for 900m along the quayside in the opposite direction to the one that you have just come, back to the Pont Saint-Esprit. Turn left and cross the Pont Mayou over the small river Nive, then turn right and follow the quayside to the expansive Place Charles de Gaulle in **Bayonne** (**61.9km, 3hr**).

BAYONNE

Bayonne is a historic, cultural and gastronomic centre for the region. Located at the confluence of the Adour and Nive rivers, it has been inhabited since

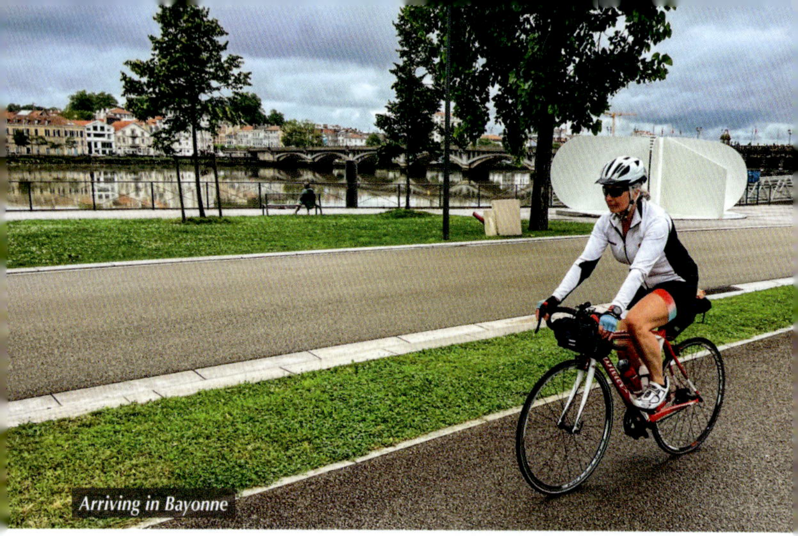

Arriving in Bayonne

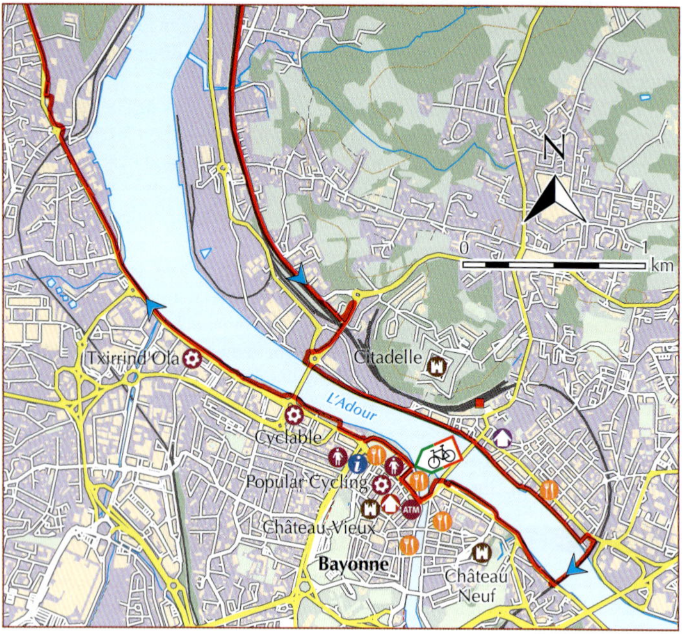

Txirrind'Ola
Cyclable
Popular Cycling
Château-Vieux
Bayonne
Château Neuf
Citadelle
L'Adour
N
0
1 km

the Middle Palaeolithic era and was the site of a Roman fort. The English controlled Bayonne from 1152 to the end of the Hundred Years' War, when it became part of France.

In the 17th century, it is claimed that the Basques of Bayonne developed the practice of fixing a knife to the end of a rifle, giving rise to the bayonet. In 1854, the railway arrived from Paris, but most tourists travelled onwards to the beaches of Biarritz. Instead, Bayonne turned to industries such as steel manufacturing, creating the industrial and post-industrial landscape that characterises the north bank of the Adour today.

Bayonne displays its Basque culture proudly, with a long-established programme of festivals and events. The most celebrated of these is the Fêtes de Bayonne, a five-day festival held annually in July. Festival-goers dress in white with a red neckerchief, and activities include a course de vaches, where cows are released into the streets of Petit Bayonne and chase, or are chased by, the crowd. A bullfight is also held in the Bayonne Arena, the largest in France, with more than 10,000 seats.

The centre of Bayonne is divided by its two rivers into three districts. The Quartier Saint-Esprit, to the north of the Adour, is connected to the rest of old Bayonne by the ancient Pont Saint-Esprit; it hosts the railway station and the massive 17th-century Vauban Citadel. To the south of the Adour, the Nive divides the town into Grand Bayonne to the west and Petit Bayonne to the east.

Petit Bayonne has narrow medieval streets of half-timbered buildings with brightly coloured shutters, many of which are now restaurants or cafés. It is home to the Musée Basque, an ethnographic museum, and to the Musée Bonnat-Helleu, which has paintings by Degas, El Greco, Botticelli and Goya. To the east of Petit Bayonne lies Château Neuf, which dates back to 1460.

Grand Bayonne is the commercial and civic hub, with its small, pedestrianised streets packed with shops, cafés and historic sites, including the 12th-century Château Vieux, home of the English Black Prince; the 13th-century Gothic Cathédrale Sainte-Marie; and the impressive Hôtel de Ville.

Bayonne is proud of its many gastronomic specialties, and it claims to be the capital of chocolate, an industry brought to the city in the 15th century by Spanish and Portuguese Jews fleeing the Alhambra Decree. Arguably, its greatest culinary offering is Bayonne Ham: a sweet, delicately flavoured dried ham that is matured for at least seven months and salted using salt from the Adour river basin. The Bayonne Ham Fair, held in April each year, is the town's oldest festival: the 2026 event was the 563rd edition!

STAGE 19

Bayonne to Hendaye

Start	Bayonne, Place Charles de Gaulle.
Finish	Hendaye, Pont de Saint-Jacques/Puente de Santiago
Time	3hr
Distance	51.7km
Ascent	490m
Descent	490m
Refreshments en route	Biarritz, Bidart, Guéthary and Saint-Jean-de-Luz
Accommodation en route	Biarritz, Bidart, Guéthary and Saint-Jean-de-Luz

The climactic stage of La Vélodyssée follows the river Adour until it meets the Atlantic and then follows the coastline south, passing sandy beaches and the glitzy resorts of Biarritz and Saint-Jean-de-Luz. Some gentle climbing with views to the Pyrenees, and the last of the French Atlantic coast, leads to Hendaye and the end of your odyssey at the Spanish border on the river Bidassoa. This is the third-shortest stage of the route, which adds to the celebratory feel. Make the most of the day – you've earned it!

From the Place Charles de Gaulle in Bayonne, head west along the quayside for 2.7km to the dock at Anglet, which contains the replica ship *L'Hermione*. Continue along Avenue de l'Adour for 2.8km, passing along the quayside of the Brise-Lames leisure marina to a roundabout. Continue straight ahead for 300m to a second

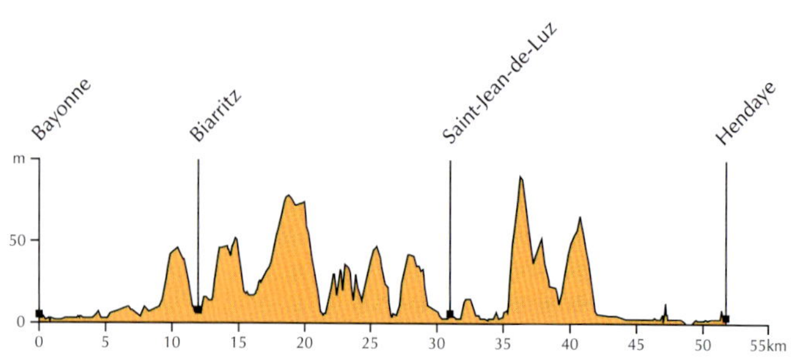

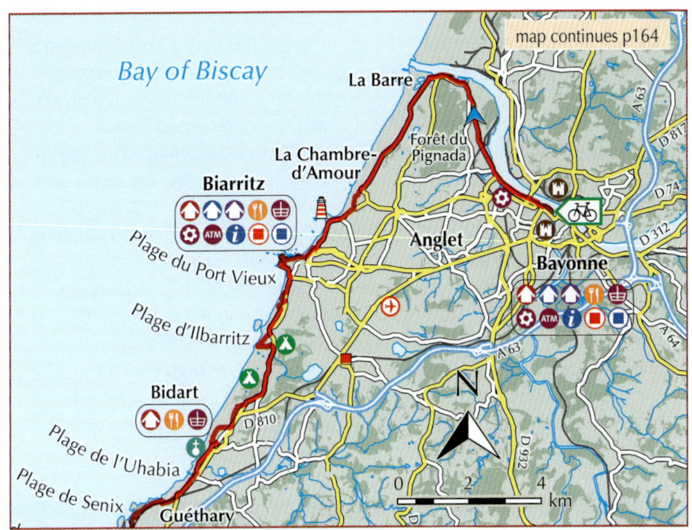

roundabout at **La Barre**. Turn left by the surfboard pedestrian crossing and follow the cycle track alongside Boulevard des Plages for 3.6km to a roundabout with a stone wall in the undeniably romantic setting of **La Chambre-d'Amour**.

Go around the roundabout, pass the first exit, then take the cycle path that leads up the hill before the second exit. Follow the cycle path through the park for 600m to reach Boulevard de la Mer. Turn right and follow the high road for 900m to the architecturally innovative Regina Experimental Hotel and the Phare de Biarritz lighthouse. Continue along Avenue de l'Impératrice for 700m to the junction with Avenue Reine Victoria. Turn right and follow the cycle lane to the Hôtel du Palais, and the seafront in **Biarritz** (**11.7km, 40min**).

BIARRITZ

Biarritz had a modest history as a port, with a small-scale whaling and fishing industry, and was quietly building a reputation as a spa resort for the European gentry when in 1854 it received a boost that ensured Biarritz would become the playground of the rich and powerful of Europe for the next 100 years. Having holidayed in Biarritz as a child, Empress Eugénie, wife of Napoleon III, persuaded the emperor to build Villa Eugénie and make it the summer home of the imperial court. It is now a luxury hotel in a spectacular location. If you are looking to splash out and celebrate completing your odyssey in opulent style, then this could be the place. It won't be cheap, but it is arguably the grandest of all the world's grand hotels.

King Edward VII found it so hard to tear himself away that when Asquith was elected British Prime Minister in 1908, he summoned the prime minister to Biarritz for the constitutional hand-kissing ceremony to avoid having to interrupt his holiday. During the 1920s, innovative art deco buildings appeared; among those that remain undiluted in their style and still perform their original function are Le Musée de la Mer, (the Biarritz Aquarium), Le Casino Municipal and the Regina Experimental and Plaza Hotels. Biarritz now claims to be the birthplace of European surfing, and the annual Biarritz Surf Festival is one of the premier longboarding events in the world.

After visiting Biarritz in 1843, Victor Hugo wrote in *Alpes et Pyrénées*, 'I do not know a place more charming and magnificent. I only have one fear: that it will become fashionable.'

Plage du Port Vieux, Biarritz

Turn left and follow Boulevard du Général de Gaulle for 500m, alongside the Grand Plage and past the casino, to the Rocher des Enfants. Follow the Boulevard du Maréchal Leclerc for 700m to the Rocher de la Vierge, where a walkway leads from the impressive art deco Musée de la Mer aquarium, through the rock and over a footbridge to the headland and the eponymous rock with the statue of the Virgin. Continue along Esplanade de la Vierge for 200m to the beautiful beach at **Plage du Port Vieux**. Go straight across the square with the car park in the middle and turn right onto Perspective de la Côte des Basques.

Follow the high road around the headland for 600m to a roundabout at the junction with Avenue de Londres. Continue along Avenue Beau Rivage, passing a roundabout with a fountain on it, for 500m, then turn right onto Avenue de Notre-Dame. Facing seawards from here, you look over Plage de la Côte des Basques, one of the world's iconic surf beaches. The neo-medieval mansion on the headland to your right is Villa Belza; in 2020, an apartment in the villa sold at a price of €40,000 per square metre. To your left you can see the looming hills of northern Spain beyond La Vélodyssée.

Continue along Avenue Notre-Dame for 300m to a roundabout. Turn sharp right onto Rue des Falaises de Beaurivage and follow the road, with similar stunning views, for 400m to Rue de Madrid. Turn right and follow the cycle lane for 800m to a roundabout. Turn right and follow Avenue Ilbarritz for 500m to the roundabout at **Plage d'Ilbarritz**.

Go straight across then turn immediately left onto a cycle track. Follow the track for 600m to a roundabout displaying Manolo Valdès's sculpture *La Dame de la Mer*. Turn right and follow the cycle lane along Avenue de la Milady for 500m to a roundabout. Go straight across and follow Avenue Biarritz for 1.4km. Bear right, following the cycle lane onto Avenue du Parc de la Reine.

Head around the small park in the middle of the road and onto Avenue des États Unis. After 100m, at the end of the road, turn left onto Rue de Tutilenia and follow for 600m to a roundabout. Bear right, then bear right again onto Corniche de la Falaise and follow for 800m to the Chapelle Sainte-Madeleine, a tiny chapel with a big view. Turn left and follow Rue de la Madeleine for 160m to the café-lined square by the church in the pretty village of **Bidart** (**20.3km, 1hr 10min**).

Make a sharp right turn, around a popular bakery-café, onto Avenue de la Grande Plage and head down the hill for 900m to a crossroads next to a beach car park at **Plage de l'Uhabia**. Turn right and then immediately left onto a cycle track that leads across a bridge over the river to a second beach car park after 300m.

Join the cycle lane beside the Avenue d'Espagne and follow it uphill for 800m to where it crosses the railway via a cycle bridge. Turn right at the end of the bridge and follow Chemin de Zubialdeko for 500m to the café-lined square in **Guéthary** (**22.8km, 1hr 20min**).

Turn right, go over the railway and then turn left onto Chemin des Falaises. Follow the road for 700m as it runs beside the railway. At a small low-ropes course, before the road crosses the railway at a level crossing, bear right and head down the hill for 200m to the beach car park at **Plage de Senix**.

Take the cycle track that leads up the hill from the far side of the car park and follow it for 600m until it meets the road by a bridge underneath the railway. Go straight across and follow Avenue Napoléon III for 800m to a T-junction. Turn left and follow Route des Plages for 300m to the beach car park at Plage de Lafitenia. Turn right and follow the road for 1.3km to **Plage d'Erromardie**.

Follow the bank of the river inland for a short distance to cross the bridge before returning to the beach. Take Chemin d'Erromardie for 600m along the beach and then uphill to a circular arena. Turn right just after the arena and continue to ascend along the cycle path and lane that leads along the clifftop, passing the botanical garden, to a roundabout after 1.4km.

The Pyrenees coming into view at Saint-Jean-de-Luz

Bear left at the roundabout and follow Rue de Sainte-Barbe for 400m, then turn right onto a cycle track and follow it towards Pointe de la Sainte-Barbe as far as the coastal track. Turn sharp left and follow the track along the beach and then Boulevard Adolphe Thiers for 1.2km to a five-way road junction. Turn right and follow Boulevard Victor Hugo for 500m to the harbour in **Saint-Jean-de-Luz** (**30.9km, 1hr 50min**).

Turn left along the quayside to the roundabout by the station. Turn right and cross the Pont Charles de Gaulle over the Nivelle river. Turn right and follow the waterfront for 2km along the quayside, past the harbour mouth, then along Boulevard Pierre Benoît to the bridge over the river Untxin at **Plage de Ciboure**.

The Route de la Corniche, which follows the coast from here, does not have a cycle lane and is not very cyclist friendly. The waymarked route heads inland and over a hill to rejoin the coast road after 6km.

Cross over the bridge and turn left onto the cycle path that runs along the bank of the river for 1.1km to the end of the basin. Turn right, then after 200m at the end of the lane by the supermarket, turn left onto Rue de Socoa. Pass under the road bridge, then after 100m, bear right at the sports centre onto Chemin d'Handiabaita. After 700m, bear right up the hill.

Follow the lane for 1.2km to a crossroads and go straight ahead onto the smaller lane. Continue for 1.9km, passing a shooting range at the top of the hill, to a road junction. Turn right to rejoin the Route de la Corniche after 700m.

Turn left and follow the cycle lane along the D912 for 2.8km to the beach at **Hendaye**. Follow the Boulevard de la Mer for 2.2km to meet the river Bidassoa at the harbour. Turn left and follow the excellent cycle path along the river for 4.6km, with sections of boardwalk above the water, to the four bridges that cross the Bidassoa at **Pont Saint-Jacques**. After passing under the two stone railway bridges, but before passing under the iron cycle bridge, there is a turning to the left that leads you to Hendaye train station in 500m. Continue along the riverbank for 2.5km, passing the historic **Île des Faisans** in the middle of the Bidassoa.

It may be hard to picture a pivotal event in European history happening here, but on the tiny muddy island of **Île des Faisans** (Island of Pheasants), in 1660, the entire Spanish court accompanied Maria Theresa, the daughter of King Philip IV of Spain, to the island to meet her prospective husband, Louis IV of France for the first time. The couple were married two days later in Saint-Jean-de-Luz. The wedding also saw the signing of the hard-won Pyrenean Peace Treaty. Over the next three centuries, the island was used as the venue for negotiating and signing numerous other treaties, leading to the island's other name, Conference Island.

It now has condominium status and is administered alternately by France and Spain, with a change of administration every six months. This is the only example in contemporary international relations of joint and alternating management of the same territory.

Just before reaching the road bridge over the river, the cycle path curves to the left and meets Rue Richelieu. Turn left, then after 100m, turn right onto Rue de l'île des Faisans. At the T-junction with Route du Capitaine Pellot, turn right and follow the road over two roundabouts and onto the Pont International (**51.7km, 3hr**). The centre of the bridge is the border with Spain and the end of La Vélodyssée.

'Happy is he who, like Odysseus, has made a beautiful journey.'
Translation of the first line of the classic French poem 'Heureux qui comme Ulysse', written by Joachim du Bellay in 1558

End of the route at Hendaye station

APPENDIX A

Accommodation

Stage	Location	Name	Type	Facilities
1	Roscoff	Camping Paradis la Pointe de Roscoff		Tent pitches, rentals, snack bar
		Hôtel d'Angleterre		Restaurant, bike storage
	Saint-Pol-de-Léon	*Camping Sunêlia la Baie de Saint Pol*		*Tent pitches, rentals, snack bar, pool*
		Camping Ar Kleguer		*Tent pitches, rentals, snack bar, pool*
		Hôtel de France		Bar, restaurant
	Morlaix	Camping Le verger de Morlaix		Tent pitches, showers
		Morlaix Youth Hostel		83 beds, restaurant
		Hôtel du Port		Bar, restaurant
	Cairhaix-Plouguer	Camping Municipal Valley of Hyère		Tent pitches, showers
		Manoir de Kerledan		4 rooms, bike storage, evening meal
		L'Écluse de l'Île		*2 rooms, bike storage, massage*
2	Gouarec	Camping Gouarec		Tent pitches, rentals, kitchen
		L'Ecrin de Bois		4 rooms, crêperie
		Abbaye de Bon-Repos B&B et Gîte		Restaurant
	Mûr-de-Bretagne	Aire Naturelle de Camping de Saint-Aignan		Tent pitches, showers
		Camping Point View		Tent pitches, rentals, showers
		Gîte de Ty Bris		3 rooms, bike storage
3	Pontivy	Camping VVF Pontivy		Tent pitches, rentals, showers

hotel B&B/guesthouse self catering hostel camping

Tel	Web/email	Comments
+33 2 98 69 70 86	camping-lapointederoscoff.fr	Family campsite with rental accommodation, near the beach
+33 2 98 69 70 42	hotel-angleterre-roscoff.fr	Rustic rooms in a low-key hotel
+33 2 98 69 06 26	camping-saintpoldeleon.com	*Family campsite next to the sea +1km east of the route*
+33 2 98 69 18 81	camping-ar-kleguer.com	*Family campsite next to the sea +1km east of the route*
+33 2 98 29 14 14	en.hotel-saint-pol.fr	Villa-style hotel with bright simple rooms.
+33 7 68 98 42 79	campinglevergerdemorlaix.wordpress.com	Quiet, rural campsite near the route
+33 2 98 15 10 55	ostal.org/votre-destination/auberge-morlaix	Good value, modern accommodation next to the route
+33 2 98 88 07 54	hotelduport-morlaix.com	Budget hotel in a 19th-century residence with river views
+33 2 98 99 10 58	campingcarhaix.wixsite.com/my-site-1	A pleasant cyclist-friendly municipal campsite by the river
+33 6 11 89 16 74	kerledan.com	B&B in a 15th-century manor house; popular with cycle tourists
+33 6 28 52 25 27	ecluse-de-lile.fr	*B&B in lock-keeper's cottage next to the route. Located 6km into Stage 2*
+33 7 68 58 19 22	campingdegouarec.com	Popular cyclist-friendly campsite next to the canal and the pretty town
+33 7 63 76 08 74	ecluse150.com	B&B and café in lock-keeper's cottage
+33 2 96 24 82 20	bon-repos.com	B&B in restored historic abbey outbuildings, next to the route
+33 2 97 27 50 20	saint-aignan56.fr	Great value municipal campsite for tents only; popular with cyclists
+33 2 96 26 01 90	camping-lepointdevue.fr	Family campsite next to the lake
+33 6 38 97 44 98	bonrepossurblavet.bzh/gîte-ty-bris	Gîte in an old station, next to the trail
+33 2 57 72 01 25	campingpontivy.fr	Cyclist-friendly family campsite

Stage	Location	Name	Type	Facilities
		Auberge de Jeunesse Pontivy		65 beds, restaurant, bike storage
		Contact Hôtel Le Rohan		Bar, lounge, restaurant
	Rohan	Camping Night & Day du Val d'Oust		Tent pitches, showers
		Villa Tranquillité		5 rooms, dinner served
	Josselin	Camping Domaine de Kerelly		Tent pitches, rentals, pool, snack bar
		Aux lits du canal		8 rooms
		Hôtel Restaurant du Château		Bar, terrace restaurant
4	Roc-Saint-andré	Domaine Du Roc		Tent pitches, rentals, snack bar, pool
	Malestroit	Domaine Les Rives de l'Oust		Tent pitches, rentals, showers
		Hôtel Cap Horn		Bar, restaurant
	Saint-Congard	Camping du Halage		Tent pitches, rentals, showers
	Saint-Martin-sur-Oust	Camping Municipal la Digue		Tent pitches, rentals, showers
	Pont d'Oust	Camping du Pont d'Oust		Tent pitches, shop, snack bar next to public swimming pool
	Vallée-de-l'Oust	Camping Painfaut		Tent pitches, rentals, showers
	Redon	Le camping de la ferme Morinais		Tent pitches, restaurant, gîte
		Hôtel Le France		Bar, restaurant, bike storage
		Hôtel Sedrez		Bar, restaurant, bike storage
5	Guenrouet	Camping St Clair		Tent pitches, rentals, showers

	Tel	Web/email	Comments
	+33 2 97 25 58 27	hifrance.org/auberges-de-jeunesse/pontivy	Hostel in a former flour mill on a small island in the heart of Pontivy, next to the route
	+33 2 97 51 11 30	lerohan-pontivy.com	Hotel in a Napoleonic mansion with straightforward modern rooms
	+33 2 97 51 57 58	night-and-day.fr/camping/33-camping-du-val-doust	Canal-side campsite, next to the route
	+33 6 76 10 12 49	villa-tranquillite.fr	Smart B&B in an elegant Belle Époque building overlooking the canal
	+33 2 97 22 22 20	camping-josselin.com	Campsite next to the river and the route
	+33 6 36 11 76 12	auxlitsducanal.fr	Good value cyclist-friendly B&B beside the canal and the trail
	+33 2 97 22 20 11	logishotels.com/fr/hotel/-890?partid=1535	Relaxed riverfront hotel with castle views
	+33 6 48 07 68 05	domaine-du-roc.fr	Family campsite beside the route and the canal
	+33 2 97 75 13 33	campingmalestroit.com	Cyclist-friendly campsite, next to the canal, a short walk to the town centre
	+33 2 97 75 13 01	hotel-malestroit.com	Simply furnished rooms with a nautical theme in an unassuming hotel
	+33 2 97 43 50 13	broceliande-vacances.com/en/offers/camping-municipal-du-halage-saint-congard/en-2280370	Pleasant campsite next to the canal in a quiet village
	+33 2 99 91 49 45	camping.info/en/campsite/camping-municipal-la-digue	Municipal campsite next to the canal and route
	+33 2 99 91 39 33	campingdupontdoust.com	Municipal campsite next to the canal and route
	+33 6 45 24 77 70	camping-lavalleedeloust.fr	Campsite next to the canal and the route
	+33 6 45 74 24 78	fermelamorinais.com	Cyclist-friendly campsite set in a tranquil farm meadow
	+33 2 99 71 06 11	hotelredon-lefrance.fr	Modest hotel with basic rooms in the centre of town
	+33 2 30 03 96 17	sedrez.fr	Comfortable modern hotel in the centre of town
	+33 2 40 87 61 52	campingsaintclair.com	Cyclist-friendly campsite near the route and the town

Stage	Location	Name	Type	Facilities
	Blain	Camping & Gîtes du Canal de Blain		Tent pitches, rentals, showers
	Nort-sur-Erdre	Camping de Port Mulon		Tent pitches, rentals, showers
		Gîte Écluse de la Tindière		3 rooms, 9 beds, bike storage, service and cleaning
		Logis Hôtel le Relais de la Grange		Bar, restaurant, bike storage
6	Nantes	Nantes Camping		Tent pitches, rentals, restaurant, indoor pool
		Le Spot - Auberge de Jeunesse		Dorms, private & family rooms, restaurant
		Radisson Blu Hotel		Bar, restaurant
7	Le Pellerin	L'Esplanade Hôtel		Bar, restaurant
		Artists' Rooms at Château du Pé		6 rooms
	Le Migron	Chambres d'hôtes Frossay/ le migron		3 rooms, bike storage
	Paimboeuf	Camping Ushuaïa Villages l'Estuaire		Tent pitches, rentals, bike village, pool
	Saint-Brevin-les-Pins	Sous les Étoiles de Paimboeuf		4 rooms
		Manoir de l'Esperance		4 rooms, tent pitches, showers, pool
		Camping Mindin		Tent pitches, rentals, snack bar, pool
8	Préfailles	Amis de la Nature		Tent pitches, showers
		Camping Eléovic		Tent pitches, rentals, snack bar, pool
	Pornic	Hôtel Beau Soleil		Bar, restaurant
	Les Moutiers-en-Retz	Camping Domaine du Collet		Tent pitches, rentals, snack bar, pool
	Bouin	La Yourte à la Ferme		Tent pitches, rental yurt

	Tel	Web/email	Comments
	+33 2 40 51 03 51	campingducanal.fr	Campsite next to the historic castle and the canal
	+33 2 36 74 82 37	night-and-day.fr/camping/35-camping-du-port-mulon	Campsite near the centre of the town, at the end of the stage
	+33 6 70 04 45 09	eclusedelatindiere.com	Very cyclist-friendly B&B in former lock-keeper's cottage
	+33 2 51 12 60 57	logishotels.com/fr/hotel/-13181?partid=1535	Clean modern rooms; popular with cyclists
	+33 2 40 74 47 94	nantes-camping.fr	Campsite in the centre of Nantes
	+33 2 19 00 32 60	cis-nantes-le-spot.com	Good value hostel in the city centre
	+33 2 72 00 10 00	radissonhotels.com/en-us/hotels/radisson-blu-nantes	Chic hotel in the imposing former Palais de Justice
	+33 2 40 04 68 14	hotel-lesplanade.fr	Uncomplicated 19th-century hotel next to the route
	+33 6 38 44 49 98	chateaudupe.fr	Part of the Estuaire art project; bedrooms turned into art installations.
	+33 6 63 26 48 16	chambres-hotes-de-la-roche.com	B&B next to the route
	+33 2 40 27 84 53	campinglestuaire.fr	Cyclist-friendly campsite next to the river and the route
	+33 6 47 01 88 78	sous-les-etoiles-de-paimboeuf.com/fr	Comfortable B&B on the route, next to the river and the art installation
	+33 6 19 26 75 80	manoirdelesperance.fr	Cyclist-friendly B&B and basic campsite for cycle tourists
	+33 2 40 27 46 41	campingmindin.com	Family campsite next to the beach
	+33 2 40 64 52 09	amis-nature.fr/hebergements/le-gite-et-le-camping-de-prefailles	Simple campsite with direct access to a quiet cove
	+33 2 40 21 61 60	camping-eleovic.com	Family campsite next to the beach and the route
	+33 2 40 82 34 58	hotel-beausoleil-pornic.com	Basic rooms in a harbour-side hotel
	+33 2 40 21 40 92	domaine-du-collet.com	Family campsite next to the beach
	+33 6 41 94 29 57	andrejeanc85.wixsite.com/yourtealaferme	Basic campsite on a farm with comfortable yurt

Stage	Location	Name	Type	Facilities
		Chambres d'hôtes Escale à Bouin		4 rooms
		Domaine le Martinet		Restaurant, bike storage, pool
9	Beauvoir-sur-Mer	Hôtel le Gois		Restaurant, indoor pool, bike storage
	Fromentine	Camping Darotte		Tent pitches, rentals, snack bar, shop, pool
		Camping Naturel les Gâts		Tent pitches, showers
	Saint-Jean-de-Monts	Camping Côté Plage		Tent pitches, rentals, snack bar, shop, pool
	Saint-Gilles-Croix-de-Vie	Camping les Cyprès		Tent pitches, rentals, snack bar, shop, pool
		Maison d'hôtes - L'envie		4 rooms, pool
		Hôtel Sea View		Bar, restaurant
	L'Île de Noirmoutier (variant route)	*Camping Les Onchères*		*Tent pitches, rentals, snack bar, pool*
		Camping Frandière		*Tent pitches, rentals, snack bar, pool*
10	Les Sables-d'Olonne	Camping le Petit Paris		Tent pitches, rentals, snack bar, pools
		Les Corderies		5 rooms
		Hôtel d'Angleterre		Bar, restaurant
	Jard-sur-Mer	Camping Paradis la Pomme de Pin		Tent pitches, rentals, snack bar, shop, pool
	La Tranche-sur-Mer	Camping Baie d'Aunis		Tent pitches, rentals, snack bar, pool
		Les Dunes Hôtel		Bar, restaurant, pool
11	L'Aiguillon-sur-Mer	Le Pré des Sables		Tent pitches, rentals, snack bar, pool
		Le Lys Blanc		Showers, bike storage
	Saint-Michel-en-l'Herm	Chambre d'hôte La Belgerie		Swimming pool

	Tel	Web/email	Comments
	+33 7 78 34 30 59	escale-a-bouin.com	Relaxed 18th-century B&B offering simple rooms plus a garden and terrace
	+33 2 51 49 23 23	domaine-lemartinet.com	A quiet hotel in an old building in the centre of the village
	+33 2 51 68 70 19	hotellegois.fr	Recently refurbished, comfortable hotel
	+33 2 51 68 53 72	campingladarotte.com	Family campsite next to the route
	+33 2 51 55 97 22	airenaturelle.com/item/85-les-gats	Simple rural campsite near to the route
	+33 2 51 58 86 58	campingcoteplage.com	Family campsite next to the route, with direct beach access
	+33 2 51 55 38 98	camping-lescypres85.co.uk	Cyclist-friendly campsite with swimming pools and direct beach access
	+33 2 28 17 04 51	maisondhotes-lenvie.fr	Comfortable B&B
	+33 2 51 55 01 91	hotelseaview.fr	A hotel with a sea view
	+33 2 51 39 81 31	les-oncheres.com	*Simple campsite near the beach*
	+33 6 83 22 62 91	camping-noirmoutier-frandiere.fr	*Simple campsite near the beach*
	+33 2 51 22 04 44	campingpetitparis.com/en	Large family campsite
	+33 6 72 77 77 83	lescorderies.fr	Tastefully decorated rooms in a comfortable B&B
	+33 2 51 21 03 28	sablesdo.com	Straightforward rooms at reasonable prices
	+33 2 51 33 43 85	campingjard.fr	Large family campsite near the beach
	+33 2 51 27 47 36	camping-baiedaunis.com	Campsite next to the main beach
	+33 2 51 30 32 27	hotel-les-dunes.com	Modest beachside hotel
	+33 2 51 27 13 88	campinglepredessables.fr	Large family campsite
	+33 6 22 32 74 10	lysblanc.fr	Cyclist-friendly guest house
	+33 6 17 79 33 34	traveleto.com/hotel/fr/chambre-d-hote-la-belgerie.html	Quiet location

Stage	Location	Name	Type	Facilities
	Marans	Camping le Bois Dinot		Tent pitches, showers, pool
		L'instant Bleu		3 rooms, massage, pool
	La Rochelle	Camping le Soleil		Tent pitches, showers
		Central - Auberge de Jeunesse et Hôtel		Dorms, rooms, restaurant, bike storage
		Un Hôtel en Ville		Bar, restaurant
12	Châtelaillon-Plage	Camping Au Port Punay		Tent pitches, rentals, snack bar, shop, pool
		Hôtel Le Rivage		Bar courtyard garden and hammam
	Saint-Lauren-de-la-Prée	Le Lagon de la Prée		Showers, restaurant and water park
	Rochefort	Camping municipal Le Rayonnement		Tent pitches, rentals
		Auberge de Jeunesse de Rochefort		Dorms, rooms, restaurant, bike storage
		Roca Fortis		Bar, restaurant, bike storage
13	Marennes	Ibis Styles Marennes Oléron		Bar, restaurant and pool
	Ronce-les-Bains	Camping Les Genets		Showers, pool, bar and restaurant
		Beach Hotel – Le Grand Chalet		Bar, restaurant and pool
	Royan	Camping de Bernezac		Tent pitches, rentals, snack bar, pool
		Hôtel Corinna		Bar, restaurant
		Family Golf Hôtel		Bar, terrace restaurant
14	Soulac-sur-Mer	Camping le Royannais		Tent pitches, rentals, snack bar, shop, pool
		L'Écume des Jours		Bar, restaurant, bike storage
	Montalivet-les-Bains	Camping Municipal du Gurp		Tent pitches, showers, rentals

	Tel	Web/email	Comments
	+33 5 46 03 15 01	naxiresav2.inaxel.com/etape1-criteres.php?compte=boisdinot	Municipal campsite
	+33 7 63 31 46 25	linstantbleu.fr	Welcoming B&B
	+33 5 46 44 42 53	aubergesdejeunesse17.fr/camping-le-soleil-la-rochelle	Cyclist-friendly campsite near the centre of town
	+33 5 79 87 02 75	centralhostel.fr/nos-destinations/la-rochelle/dortoir-la-rochelle	Youth hostel in an old building in the centre of town
	+33 5 46 41 15 75	unhotelenville.com	A relaxed small hotel in the centre of town
	+33 5 17 81 00 00	camping-port-punay.com/en	Comfortable campsite next to the route
	+33 5 46 56 25 79	hotel-lerivage.com	Low-key rooms, some with kitchenettes, in a modest hotel with bay views
	+33 5 46 84 89 40	lagondelapree.com/en	Large family campsite
	+33 5 46 82 67 70	camping-le-rayonnement.fr	Bike-friendly campsite
	+33 5 46 99 74 62	aubergesdejeunesse17.fr/rochefort	Modern youth hostel
	+33 5 46 26 99 32	hotelrocafortis.fr	Comfortable hotel in historic dockyard
	+33 5 46 75 98 89	all.accor.com/hotel/9493/index.en.shtml	Chain hotel near the route
	+33 5 46 36 08 45	atlantique-genets.fr	Large family campsite near the route and beach
	+33 5 46 36 06 41	le-grand-chalet.fr	Hotel with great sea views
	+33 5 46 39 00 71	en.bernezac.acccf.com	Campsite on the edge of town and near the beach
	+33 5 46 39 82 53	hotel-corinna.fr	Relaxed hotel in a 1950s building with simple rooms
	+33 5 46 05 14 66	family-golf-hotel.com/en	Whitewashed beachfront hotel with sea view
	+33 5 56 09 61 12	royannais.com/en	Quiet cyclist-friendly campsite
	+33 5 56 09 81 34	hotelecumedesjours.fr	Simple hotel near the route
	+33 5 56 09 44 53	campinglegurp.com	Cyclist-friendly municipal campsite next to the beach and the route.

Stage	Location	Name	Type	Facilities
	Plage du Pin Sec	Camping municipal du Pin Sec		Tent pitches, showers
	Hourtin Plage	Camping de la Côte d'Argent		Tent pitches, rentals, snack bar, shop, pool
	Carcans Plage	Camping de l'Océan Carcans		Tent pitches, showers
	Maubuisson	Camping de Maubuisson		Tent pitches, rentals, snack bar, pools
	Lacanau-Océan	Yelloh Village Les Grands Pins		Tent pitches, rentals, snack bar, shop, pool
		La Côte d'Argent		Bar, restaurant
15	Le Porge-Océan	Camping Municipal la Grigne		Tent pitches, showers
	Le Grand Crohot	Camping Brémontier		Tent pitches, rentals
	Andernos-les-Bains	Camping Fontaine Vieille		Tent pitches, rentals, snack bar, shop, pool
	Biganos	Camping le Marache Vacances		Tent pitches, rentals, snack bar
	Arcachon	Hutopia Arcachon		Tent pitches, rentals, bar, restaurant, shop, pools
		Camping municipal de Verdalle		Tent pitches, rentals, shop
		Hôtel Ville d'Hiver		Bar, restaurant
16	Dune du Pilat	Camping Village Panorama du Pyla		Tent pitches, rentals, snack bar, water park
		Hôtel Restaurant La Co(o)rniche		Bar, restaurant, indoor pool
	Biscarrosse Plage	Camping Le Vivier		Tent pitches, rentals, snack bar, shop, pool
		Hôtel Les Vagues		Bar, restaurant
		Le Grand Hôtel and Restaurant de la Plage		Bar, restaurant, outdoor infinity pool
	Navarrosse	Camping de Navarrosse		Tent pitches, rentals, snack bar, shop, pool
		Hôtel Côte et Lac		Bar, restaurant, pool

Tel	Web/email	Comments
+33 5 56 73 00 66	pin-sec.com/en	Municipal campsite next to the beach
+33 5 56 09 10 25	camping-cote-dargent.com	Family campsite next to the beach and route
+33 5 56 03 41 44	camping-carcans-ocean.com	Cyclist-friendly municipal campsite
+33 5 56 03 30 12	camping-maubuisson.com	Campsite near lakeside beach
+33 5 56 03 20 77	lesgrandspins.com/en	Family friendly campsite with outdoor pool
+33 5 56 03 21 58	hotel-lacanau.fr	Basic rooms, with balconies overlooking the beach
+33 5 56 26 54 88	camping-leporge.fr	Municipal campsite next to the route and the beach
+33 5 56 60 03 99	campingbremontier.fr/en	Family-run campsite among the pine trees
+33 5 56 82 01 67	fontainevieille.fr	Campsite next to the beach
+33 5 57 70 61 19	marachevacances.com	Family campsite with pool and bar
+33 5 64 09 10 13	europe.huttopia.com/site/arcachon	Campsite near the centre of town
+33 5 56 66 12 62	campingdeverdalle.com	Municipal campsite next to the route and the beach
+33 5 56 66 10 36	hotelvilledhiver.com	Elegant hotel with pool in a 19th-century water storage facility
+33 5 56 22 10 44	camping-panorama.com	Tranquil pine-shaded family campsite with access to the beach
+33 5 56 22 72 11	lacoorniche.com	Smart hotel with views across the bay
+33 5 58 78 25 76	ms-vacances.com/camping-campeole/camping-le-vivier	Family campsite near the beach and route
+33 5 58 83 98 10	lesvagues.com	Informal hotel near the beach and the route
+33 5 58 82 74 00	legrandhoteldelaplage.fr	Smart modern rooms with ocean views
+33 5 58 09 84 32	https://www.campeole.com/fr/camping/navarrosse	Campsite next to the route and the lakeside beach
+33 5 58 09 83 13	cote-et-lac.com	Quaint informal hotel next to the route

Stage	Location	Name	Type	Facilities
	Biscarrosse	Hotel Atlantide		Terrace, lounge and bar
	Parentis-en-Born	Camping Au Lac de Biscarrosse		Tent pitches, rentals, bar restaurant, shop, pools
		The Originals Boutique Hôtel		Bar, restaurant
	Gastes	Les Prés Verts		Tent pitches, rentals, bar, restaurant, shop, pools
		Les Echasses		Tent pitches, rentals, showers
		Le Camping Municipal du Lac		Tent pitches, rentals, pool
17	Mimizan Plage	Siblu Camping La Plage		Tent pitches, rentals, snack bar, shop, pool
		Hôtel Atlantique		Bar, restaurant
	Contis Plage	Lous Seurrots		Tent pitches, rentals, snack bar, shop, water park
		Hôtel Côté Phare		Bar, restaurant
		Hôtel de la Plage		Bar, seafood restaurant
	Cap de l'Homy	Camping municipal du Cap de l'Homy		Tent pitches, rentals, showers
	Saint-Girons-Plage	Les Tourterelles		Tent pitches, rentals, bar, restaurant, shop, pools
	Léon	Le Col Vert		Tent pitches, rentals, bar, restaurant, shop, pools
		Le Fair Play		Bar, restaurant
18	Moliets-et-Maa	Logis Hôtel de l'Océan		Terrace, bar and restaurant
	Vieux-Boucau-les-Bains	Camping les Chênes		Tent pitches, rentals, snack bar
		Atlantic Surf Lodge Hostel		Bar, restaurant
	Le Penon	Siblu Camping les Oyats		Tent pitches, rentals, bar, restaurant, shop, pools
	Hossegor	Jo&Joe Hostel		Dorms, rooms, bar, restaurant, lounge
		Les Fougères		Bar, restaurant, pool, garden

	Tel	Web/email	Comments
	+33 5 58 78 08 86	hotelatlantide.fr	Basic hotel in the town, near the route
	+33 5 58 08 06 40	camping-lac-de-biscarrosse.com/fr	Large family campsite next to the lake
	+33 5 58 78 41 05	hotel-lakeside.com	Lakeside hotel and restaurant
	+33 5 58 09 74 11	presverts.net	Cyclist-friendly campsite next to the lake, at the end of the stage
	+33 5 58 09 31 76	campinglesechasses.com	Large family campsite next to the route
	+33 5 58 09 70 10	lecampingdulac.com	Municipal campsite next to the lake and the route
	+33 5 58 09 00 32	siblu.fr	Large family campsite near and next to the route
	+33 5 58 09 09 42	atlantique-mimizan.fr	Straightforward lodging with a terrace and sea views
	+33 5 58 42 85 82	lous-seurrots.com/en	Large family campsite
	+33 5 58 74 34 72	hotelcotepharecontis.com	Simple rooms in cyclist-friendly hotel
	+33 6 77 38 28 71	hotelplagecontis.com	Stylish rooms with local art
	+33 5 58 42 83 47	camping-cap.com/en	Municipal beachside campsite
	+33 5 58 47 93 12	campeole.com/etablissement/post/les-tourterelles-vielle-saint-girons	Large family campsite next to the beach and route
	+33 4 11 32 90 00	sandaya.fr/camping/france/aquitaine/le-col-vert	Campsite next to the lake and route
	+33 5 58 90 44 94	fairplay-leon.fr	Unpretentious hotel
	+33 5 58 48 51 19	l-ocean.fr	Simple hotel next to the beach
	+33 5 58 48 21 21	campingleschenes.fr/hebergements-nuit-velodyssee	Cyclist-friendly campsite next to the route; excellent value for cycle tourists.
	+33 5 58 48 31 37	atlantic-surflodge.com	Relaxed hostel
	+33 5 58 73 53 96	siblu.fr	Large family campsite
	+33 5 58 35 68 55	joandjoe.com/hossegor/en	Well-maintained hostel near the centre of town
	+33 5 58 43 78 00	hotel-lesfougeres.fr	Simple hotel

Stage	Location	Name	Type	Facilities
	Labenne-Océan	Camping les Pins Bleus		Tent pitches, rentals, pool
	Bayonne	Hostel20 Bayonne		Dorms, rooms, apartments, kitchen, lounge
		Hôtel des Arceaux		Bar, restaurant
		Le Grand Hôtel, Bayonne		Bar, restaurant
19	Biarritz	Biarritz Camping		Tent pitches, rentals, bar, restaurant, pool
		Coast-Utopy Hostel		Dorms, rooms, kitchen, lounge
		Hôtel Regina Experimental		Bar, restaurant, pool
	Bidart	Camping de la Plage		Tent pitches, showers
		Hôtel du Fronton		Bar, terrace restaurant
	Guéthary	Chibau Berria - Camping Municipal		Tent pitches, showers
		L'escale Surf Hostel		15 beds, dorms, room, kitchen, bike storage
		Hôtel Villa Catarie		Bar, restaurant, pool, garden
	Saint-Jean-de-Luz	Camping le Bord de Mer		Tent pitches, showers
		Hôtel de Paris		Bar, restaurant
		Grand Hôtel Spa & Thalasso		Bar, restaurant, spa, pool
	Hendaye	Camping Alturan		Tent pitches, showers
		Demain c'est loin		Dorms, rooms, bar, restaurant
		Hôtel Santiago		Bar, restaurant, pool

Tel	Web/email	Comments
+33 5 59 45 41 13	lespinsbleus.com/en	Cyclist-friendly municipal campsite next to the route
+33 5 59 64 65 75	hostel20-bayonne.com	Relaxed hostel near the city centre
+33 5 59 59 15 53	hotelarceaux.fr	Budget hotel with shared bathroom in an old building in the city centre.
+33 5 59 59 62 00	all.accor.com/hotel/A0Y1/index.en.shtml	Smart chain hotel in the city centre
+33 5 59 23 00 12	biarritz-camping.fr	Campsite on the edge of town, close to route and beach
+33 7 49 19 84 63	utopyhostel.com	Comfortable hostel next to the route and near the sea
+33 5 59 41 33 00	en.reginaexperimental.com	Chic Belle Époque hotel with grand atrium and vintage surfboards on the walls
+33 9 72 37 09 08	laplage.ovh	Quiet cyclist-friendly campsite with simple facilities, next to the beach and route
+33 5 59 54 72 76	hoteldufronton.com	Hotel, bar and restaurant on the pretty town square; views over the hills and the ocean
+33 5 59 26 11 94	camping-saintjeandeluz.fr/en	Straightforward municipal campsite next to the route and the sea
+33 6 51 91 39 73	lescalesurfhostelguethary.com	Cyclist-friendly hostel near to the route
+33 5 40 07 81 88	villa-catarie.com/en	Cosy rooms in a traditional Basque villa
+33 5 59 26 24 61	camping-le-bord-de-mer.fr/en	Small campsite next to the sea and the route.
+33 5 59 51 03 44	hotel-saintjeandeluz.brithotel.com	Budget hotel with nautical-themed rooms, next to the route and the station
+33 5 59 26 35 36	luzgrandhotel.fr/en	Refined hotel with 1930s-inspired rooms next to the beach and route
+33 5 59 20 04 55	camping-alturan.com	Simple campsite, ideal for tents, on the edge of town
+33 5 59 06 80 69	hostel-hendaye.fr	Cyclist-friendly hostel near the end of the route and the train station
+33 5 59 20 00 94	hotel-le-santiago.com	Unassuming hotel near the end of the route and the train station.

APPENDIX B

What to take

The following list is for camping using bikepacking bags. Weights are offered as a guide only.

Item	Weight (g)
Camping	
Tent	1500
Sleeping bag	1000
Sleeping mat	700
Stove	250
Pan	100
Bowl	100
Spork	10
Penknife	100
Head torch	100
Bike	
Handlebar bag	350
Seat post bag	600
Frame bag	400
Tool kit	300
Spare tube and levers	250
Bike lock	100
Drink bottle	100
Pump	100
Front light	100
Rear light	50
Bell	10
Consumables	
Trail food	
Toilet paper	
Gas cylinder	

Item	Weight (g)
Clothes (carried)	
Waterproof jacket	400
Down jacket/fleece top	500
Spare base layer top	150
Spare trousers	150
Spare socks and underwear	150
Spare footwear	
Other kit	
This guidebook	300
Phone	150
Passport and wallet	100
Wash kit	350
Travel towel	100
First aid kit	150
Charger cables	50
Power bank	150
Clothes (wearing)	
Cycle helmet	260
Base layer top	250
Cycle top with rear pockets	500
Padded bib shorts/trousers	250
Socks	50
Cycling shoes	800
Cycle gloves	150
Sunglasses	50
Watch	50

At the triangular Quai Valin, La Rochelle (Stage 11)

For winter, replace sunhat with warm hat, shorts with long trousers or add leg warmers, and cycling gloves with warm gloves. Add a fleece or lightweight down jacket and lightweight, breathable waterproof over-trousers. Cycling shoes that fix to your pedals are more efficient for cycling than trainers but can be scary if you are not used to them. However, trainers are more practical to double up as non-cycling shoes.

Your wash kit should be kept to a minimum: include toilet paper and detergent for washing clothes. A wet razor and manual toothbrush are lighter than their electric equivalents. If you are not cycling alone, consider sharing some items, such as toothpaste and shampoo.

A bike repair kit should include the ability to repair a puncture depending on your type of tyres, tyre levers, chain lube, a multitool, spoke key and chain-link tool. If using tubeless tyres, consider a compressed-gas tyre inflator; spare inner-tubes can also be fitted in tubeless tyres if needed.

A first aid kit can be small but should include nitrile gloves, antiseptic wipes, antiseptic cream, plasters, bandages and anti-inflammatory tablets. Also include any medication that you take regularly in sufficient quantity for the duration of trip.

Some people choose to carry a heavy-duty bike lock, and some carry a thinner but lighter-weight one. The argument for the second is that they are secure enough to deter opportunist thieves but would be equally ineffective as a heavy-duty lock to a determined one.

APPENDIX C

Useful contacts

Transport

Brittany Ferries (UK)
tel +44 330 159 7000
brittany-ferries.co.uk

Brittany Ferries (Ireland)
tel +353 021 427 7801
brittany-ferries.ie

SNCF (French Railways)
tel +33 1 84 91 91 91
sncf-connect.com

Eurostar
tel +44 3432 186186
eurostar.com

European Bike Express
tel +44 1430 422877
bike-express.co.uk

Cycling organisations

Cycling UK (Formerly Cyclists' Touring Club)
tel +44 1483 238300
cyclinguk.org

Maps and guides

La Vélodyssée route guide
cycling-lavelodyssee.com

EuroVelo EV1 route guide
en.eurovelo.com/ev1

OpenStreetMap (free online mapping)
openstreetmap.org

Komoot (cycling navigation app)
komoot.com

Stanfords (map shop)
7 Mercer Walk, London WC2H 9FA
tel +44 20 7836 1321
stanfords.co.uk

Accommodation

Warm Showers (free accommodation offered to cyclists)
warmshowers.org

France Vélo Tourisme (similar to Cyclists Welcome in the UK)
en.francevelotourisme.com

Hostelling International (youth hostel bookings)
hihostels.com

Gîtes d'étapes guide (youth hostel accommodation)
gites-refuges.com

Airbnb (accommodation-finding app)
airbnb.co.uk

APPENDIX D

Links to other cycle routes

The EuroVelo 1

An 11,000km cycle route from North Cape in Norway to Sagres in Portugal. La Vélodyssée forms the French part of this route.

NCN Devon Coast to Coast

Meets La Vélodyssée at Roscoff at the start of Stage 1 after a ferry crossing from Plymouth. It runs for 158km, from Ilfracombe to Plymouth, and forms the South-West England part of EuroVelo 1.

Redon to Saint-Malo

Meets La Vélodyssée at Redon at the end of Stage 4 and follows voies vertes for 190km to the ferry port in St Malo.

River Loire Cycle Route

Meets La Vélodyssée at Nantes at the end of Stage 6. The route follows the river Loire for 1,062km, from its source at Mont Gerbier de Jonc to its mouth at Saint-Nazaire.

La Vélo Francette

Meets La Vélodyssée at La Rochelle at the end of Stage 11 and follows voies vertes and quiet lanes for 600km to the ferry port at Ouistreham in Normandy.

Le Canal des Deux Mers à Vélo

Meets La Vélodyssée at Royan at the end of Stage 13 and follows canals for 690km to Sète on the French south coast, linking the Atlantic to the Mediterranean.

The Camino de Santiago

Links to La Vélodyssée via a 63km ride along the river Nive, from Bayonne at the end of Stage 18 to St Jean-Pied-de-Port. It then follows the historic pilgrimage route for 770km to Santiago de Compostela in northern Spain.

Hendaye to Bilbao

Links to La Vélodyssée at Hendaye at the end of Stage 19. This route, which is not waymarked and has significantly more hills and fewer cycleways than La Vélodyssée, continues along the beautiful northern coast of Spain for 160km to Bilbao, where you can then take a ferry back to Plymouth.

Other cycle routes

A vast web of regional waymarked cycleways interconnect with La Vélodyssée and increase the potential for personalising and enriching your adventure. You can obtain local maps from tourist information offices; alternatively, IGN Greenways and Cycle Routes Map 924 cover the whole of France.

APPENDIX E

Language glossary

English	French
yes	*oui*
no	*non*
please	*s'il vous plait*
thank you	*merci*
hello	*bonjour*
good bye	*au revoir*
good evening	*bon soir*
sorry	*pardon*
are you ok?	*ça va?*
I am fine/ I am well	*ça va/ça va bien*
I would like	*je voudrais*
I understand	*je comprends*
I don't understand	*je ne comprends pas*
look out!	*attention!*

English	French
bike	*le vélo*
cyclist	*le cycliste*
puncture	*la crevaison*
brake	*le frein*
wheel	*la roue*
tyre	*le pneu*
gears	*les vitesses*
spokes	*les rayons*
chain	*la chaîne*
where is...?	*oú est...?*
the station	*la gare*
tourist office	*l'office de tourism (m)*
youth hostel	*l'auberge de jeunesse (f)*
the bill	*l'addition (m)*
a glass of water	*un verre d'eau*

French	English
la viande	meat
la véloroute	long-distance cycle route
la voie verte	traffic-free cycleway/ bridleway
l'écluse (f)	lock (on a canal)
le pont	bridge
le quai	quay
le chemin de halage	towpath
le marais	marshland
le gîte	holiday home
le château	castle/big house
le fort	fort
l'église (f)	church
la mairie	town hall
l'hôtel de ville	city hall
le barrage	dam
le chemin de fer	railway
entrée interdite	no entry

French	English
la route fermée	road closed
la déviation	diversion
sens unique	one-way street
sauf vélo	except cycles
tournez á gauche/ droite	turn left/right
tout droit	straight on
la forêt	forest
les bois	woods
le plat du jour	dish of the day
la carte	the menu
un café allongé	a long black coffee
au lait	with milk
une bière pression	draft beer
nos vins rouges	our red wines
nos vins blancs	our white wines
l'étang	pond (lake)
le poisson	fish

The Cicerone range

International walking & trekking

British walking & long distance

Pilgrimages

Short walks

Via ferrata, climbing & scrambling

Cycling, mountain biking & bikepacking

Winter climbs & snow sports

Trail & fell running

Our formats

App

A digitised version of the guidebook's expert-curated routes, with interactive maps, detailed facilities information and offline GPS navigation

Guidebook

The complete guidebook with detailed descriptions, route and facilities information, profiles and maps in an easy-to-use printed format

eBook

The digital edition of the guidebook with detailed descriptions, route and facilities information, profiles and maps, ready to use on any device

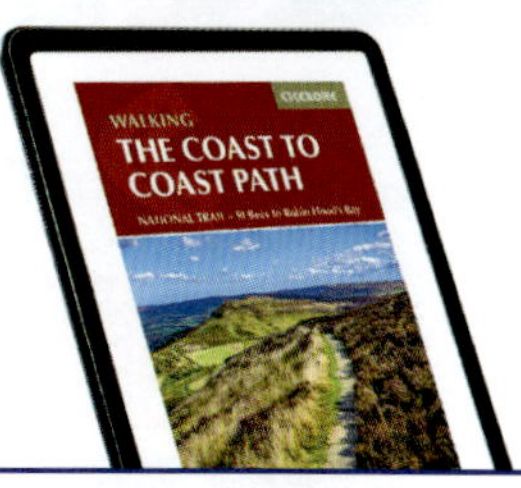

GPX files

Download GPX route files from your account to use on compatible devices for easy navigation and planning

See available formats for this book at **cicerone.co.uk/1274**

GPX files

Download free GPX files for this book

cicerone.co.uk/1274/GPX

Other cycle touring guides

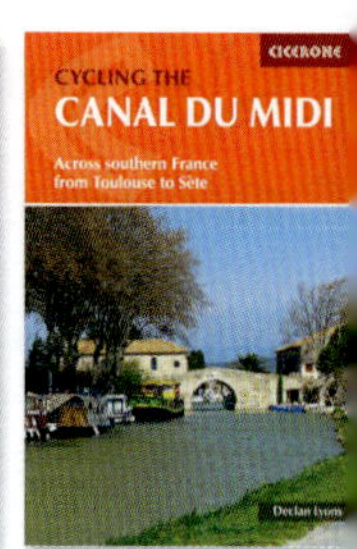

Other guides to this region

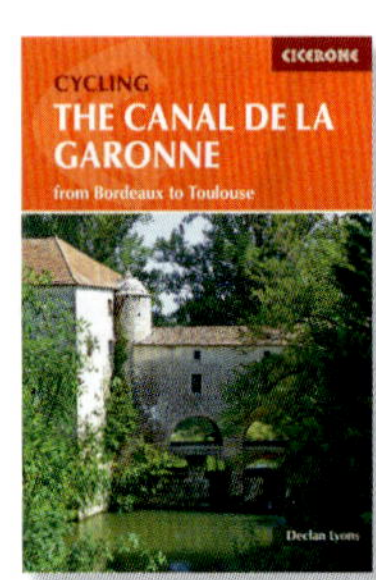

Trust Cicerone to guide your next adventure

cicerone.co.uk